PUNCHING NAZIS

PUNCHING NAZIS

and other good ideas

KEITH LOWELL JENSEN

Skyhorse Publishing

Skyhorse Publishing books may be purchased in bulk at special discounts for sales promotion, corporate gifts, fund-raising, or educational purposes. Special editions can also be created to specifications. For details, contact the Special Sales Department, Skyhorse Publishing, 307 West 36th Street, 11th Floor, New York, NY 10018 or info@skyhorsepublishing.com.

Skyhorse® and Skyhorse Publishing® are registered trademarks of Skyhorse Publishing, Inc.®, a Delaware corporation.

Visit our website at www.skyhorsepublishing.com.

10 9 8 7 6 5 4 3 2 1

Library of Congress Cataloging-in-Publication Data is available on file.

Cover design by Erin Seaward-Hiatt
Cover Photograph: IStock

Print ISBN: 978-1-5107-3374-9
Ebook ISBN: 978-1-5107-3375-6

Printed in the United States of America

CONTENTS

To Mom and Dad, for encouraging my creative efforts and for teaching me that racists are the worst. .

Trigger-Warning Warning
The next page contains a trigger warning.

TRIGGER WARNING

This book is full of descriptions of bigotry, violence, and hate speech, and the forty-fifth President of the United States is mentioned several times by name. I tell you this, dear reader, so that you may make an informed decision as to where and when you read it, or whether to read it at all.

When I shared an article online that contained graphic descriptions of violence, I included a trigger warning. Immediately a fan messaged me. "Dude, trigger warnings? You're a comedian. Cut that shit out."

I asked what was wrong with trigger warnings and what this had to do with me being a comedian.

"Being a comedian and fighting for free speech go hand in hand. You're giving power to people who will stop you from speaking your mind down the road."

I'm amazed how often I'm told what I can or cannot say by champions of free speech. I argued that trigger warnings made me feel freer to speak my mind, allowing me to do so without worrying about triggering my friends who have survived trauma and who live with PTSD.

I pointed out that NPR always tells listeners if a story is going to be graphic in depictions of violence, which is handy when you drive around with kids in your car.

"There are sad songs that make me cry. Should they put warnings on them?"

When I explained that crying from a sad song was a little different from having a strong reaction after surviving a war zone or being sexually assaulted, the guy started to get angrier. He insulted me, he made ad hominem attacks, he became increasingly irrational.

I started to feel bad that I had upset the guy, especially since he had been a supportive fan of my comedy. I told him that I was really sorry that the trigger warning had affected him, and I promised him that in the future, to avoid repeating this situation, I'd give him some kind of warning to let him know when I was about to post a trigger warning.

SUICIDAL

"I'm Suicidial."

It was a surprising thing for Jamie to be confiding to me just minutes into seeing each other for the first time in years. We'd both become legal adults since we'd last hung out. Riding in his beautiful, tricked-out, low-rider pickup truck, we were speeding at ninety-plus miles per hour down the 91 in Corona, California, my old hometown.

My buddy Dan had made the trip from Sacramento with me. There wasn't room in the cab of the truck for him, so he was lying down in the bed, no doubt in the grip of terror.

"You're suicidal? Dude, I'm sorry. What's going on?" I asked, wishing he hadn't told me this while behind the wheel of a fast-moving truck with no seat belts and one of my dear friends in the bed.

"No, homes, I'm not suicidal, I'm Suicidal. I'm a fuckin' Suey, man."

"You're a suicidal person? You want to die?" I asked, still not comprehending but admittedly a little impressed. It's wrong, I know, but as someone with suicidal impulses myself, I associate

1

a certain depth of character with wanting to take one's own life. When I hear of someone killing him- or herself, who I initially hadn't thought much of, I reconsider my opinion of them. In the instances where it turns out to be accidental death by autoerotic asphyxiation, I think, "Yeah, that makes more sense."

Jamie rolled his eyes, took one hand off the polished wood steering wheel, and pulled his shirt up to reveal "Suicidal" tattooed across his abs in Old English lettering. "I'm Suicidal."

After a few more clueless questions I finally was able to understand that Jamie had become a member of a local gang called the Suicidals.

I'd moved up north to Sacramento with my parents when I was fourteen, leaving behind Jamie, my best friend in Corona, which is about an hour drive inland from Los Angeles. I barely recognized him now, buff, covered in tattoos, a far cry from the towheaded, blue-eyed Ricky Schroder look-alike who I used to listen to The Cure with.

I associated my friendship with Jamie with a sort of eighties take on Tom Sawyer and Huck Finn, full of mischievous anecdotes like the time we'd gone to Christian summer camp together and Jamie got caught shoplifting Lemonheads from a grocery store on the way home, humiliating but not surprising my mom. Apparently, he hadn't been as moved by the Holy Spirit as I was. Camp had affected me deeply—at one point I even tried to burn my Pink Floyd cassette tapes. Jamie was not quite so taken in.

Now it was the early nineties and his appearance suggested a darker kind of mischief.

It seems a big change had happened in Home Gardens—the neighborhood I'd spent the first decade and a half of my life in— after I'd left. The best I can figure is that the LA gang sweeps pushed the gangs into the Inland Empire, and they settled there, the same way the ocean winds pushed the LA smog onto us.

There'd always been some tension between the white kids and the Mexican kids in Corona. When I lived in Home Gardens, we only had about five black kids, so they were almost celebrities to us, able to move between cliques, welcome by most. But in the late eighties with the black gangs coming in, the original white and Mexican residents banded together, a bizarre hybrid of skateboarding, speed-metal-loving, racist cholo rockers. I guessed they'd taken their name from the band Suicidal Tendencies, but it seemed pretty square to ask.

In addition to joining a gang, my childhood pal had become a drug dealer, and a rather successful one judging by the truck we were in; the Impala and the Jet Ski parked in his mom's driveway next to the van he'd bought her; and the impressive collection of guns at the apartment he rented for storing his drugs (so that his mom wouldn't lose her house if he got busted, he explained) and for having sex, because, obviously.

Jamie made several stops at pay phones around town to arrange to pick up cash, which, we learned, was done separately from delivering drugs. At each stop I checked with Dan to see how he was doing, and remarkably, he seemed pretty okay with riding in the bed of an erratically driven truck on drug-dealing errands.

Dan was the half-Jewish, half-Irish son of a lawyer. He had long, curly red hair that hung in his face and made me think of the incredibly handsome lead singer of Simply Red, and thick glasses that did not make me think of the incredibly handsome lead singer of Simply Red at all. Dan was the kind of friend who turned you onto Henry Miller's books and cool bands like Dinosaur Jr., The Pixies, and Galaxie 500. I assumed he must be

3

losing his mind at this rather extreme introduction to my hometown, but he was being an adventure tourist and taking it all in stride.

Jamie jumped back behind the wheel. "Alright, I'm done doin' business for now. Let's go grab Psycho and have some beers."

"Psycho?" I asked, not sure if we'd be grabbing a human being or some new designer drug.

"Yeah, he's cool," Jamie answered.

We pulled up in front of a house I knew well—the home of my childhood friend Eric. We were now on the block I grew up on. "Did Eric change his name to Psycho?"

"What? No, stupid. Psycho just stays here." Jamie hopped out of his truck and kicked the bushes in front of Eric's house. A muscular Mexican man climbed out of the bushes groggily, but with quick enough reflexes to catch the case of beer Jamie tossed at his head.

Dan and I were introduced to Psycho. We said hello. He stared at us, hard and without a word.

I decided to cut the tension by knocking on Eric's door to see if he was around. Eric's mother, with her thick German accent, recognized me immediately and was excited to see me. "Kees! How are you? Eric, come, it is Kees!" By contrast, Eric, who I hadn't seen in over five years, since we were kids, greeted me as if we'd seen each other the day before, and every day prior to that. "Hey, what's up, dude?" he asked, as he walked out the door and past me.

We joined the group now standing around on Eric's driveway. Seeing Dan drinking day beers with Jamie and Psycho gave me a giggle. I cracked a beer and noticed Psycho glaring at me again.

"Hey Jamie," he started, his eyes locked on me. "Why we hanging out with a skinhead?"

"Me?" I stammered, looking around for someone to defend me. "No. I'm not a skinhead. I've never been a skinhead. I just cut my hair short because it's hot out, and it's not even that short. Skinhead? No. No, sir, absolutely not." As he continued staring right through me, I continued rambling desperately. "I listen to The Cure. Skinheads don't listen to The Cure. Jamie, tell him, tell him I listen to The Cure."

Psycho's attitude toward me did not soften, no matter how much I joked with the group and got laughs from the other three. He kept coming back to: "Why are we hanging out with a skinhead? I'm not cool with hanging out with a skinhead."

A few cans of beer later and I had the bright idea to just tackle this head on. I attempted to reason with Psycho. I decided to reason . . . with Psycho.

"Look, Psycho, I grew up here, right on this street. I've known these two guys since we were tots. What can I do to prove to you that I am not a skinhead?"

"You want to prove you're down?"

"Yes! That's it exactly. Well put. I am down. How can I prove it?"

"Fight me."

"What?!"

"Fight me. That'll prove you're down."

I was aghast to hear myself answering, "Oh . . . kay. Let's fight then, because I'm down . . . " I think maybe I thought that just agreeing would prove my down-ness without me having to actually go through with it. As it became clear that Psycho was ready to brawl, my sense of self-preservation, which was apparently off daydreaming when the previous words were spoken, kicked in, and I added, "But no hitting in the face or in the nuts, deal?"

"Yeah, sure," a man named Psycho who lived in a bush agreed, as I prepared to fight him.

We squared off, fists up. I jabbed and he took the hit like I imagine a cinder block might. He threw a punch and I got my shoulder in front of it to block. My shoulder screamed in pain and informed the rest of my body it was on its own from here on out. I jabbed again, and again did no damage. We circled around each other exchanging punches, feeling each other out, and probably giving me impressive bruises on both arms.

Then I got my shot. Psycho threw a punch and I managed to not only dodge it, but to catch his right arm between my chest and my left arm. I pushed up with my forearm against his elbow, locking his arm between my forearm and my armpit. With my right I started driving uppercuts into his ribs with everything I had. I punched him so many times and with such force that I was sure he was done. I can only imagine that if I'd been receiving these same punches my ribs would be cracked in several places. When I let go of his arm it was an act of mercy. I let go so that he could drop to the ground, and maybe receive help, some ice from Eric's kitchen at least, perhaps a ride to the emergency room. I hoped he would not need an ambulance.

Psycho did not drop. He took his arm back, staying perfectly upright, and stared at me. Then to my absolute terror, he smiled. He smiled for the first time that day and said, sarcastically, "Ouch!" He punched me in the chest so hard I hit the ground. As I lay there gasping for breath he said the most beautiful three words I'd ever heard: "Yeah, he's down."

I was down. It was true in at least two senses of the word. Jamie was laughing hard as he helped me up and handed me a beer. Then he decided this was too much fun to miss out on.

"I want to fight you now!"

I'd beaten Jamie up many times when we were kids. I understood him wanting a chance to be on the other end, and in fact I was feeling a bit of the same after the humiliating beating I'd just taken and I idiotically agreed to fight him.

"Same rules. No hitting in the face and no hitting in the balls." We squared up, fists raised. I jabbed. Jamie dodged and punched me hard in the nuts. I hit the ground a second time. "There ain't no rules in fighting, bitch." He helped me to my feet again and again handed me a beer, laughing cheerily.

I was done fighting for the day.

Psycho now had his eye on Dan. "Hey, I don't know you. You down?"

Dan then earned my eternal respect as he calmly responded, "Yes, Psycho," the moniker sounding unnatural coming from his mouth. "I would of course love a chance to prove that I'm down, and I definitely am, but I can't fight you because I'm Jewish."

Not, "I'm Jewish and we're not allowed to fight on Saturday" or anything like that, just "I'm Jewish." Which, delightfully, had the effect of eliciting a bewildered stare followed by, "Yeah, this dude's down." Psycho put his arm around Dan. More beers were drunk.

We went by Jamie's apartment after switching vehicles so that everyone could enjoy the relative safety of a seat belt as we sped erratically over to the "office" to grab some weed. He had refrigerators full of marijuana, more weed than I'd ever seen in one place.

Dan was doing a great job of "When in Rome," handling Jamie's guns and admiring his vast collection of pornography.

Jamie had some more friends he wanted to introduce us to. We made a swing through a fast-food drive-through and then drove out to the middle of a large, empty field for a small, impromptu party. Dan had a fancy new pipe with a resin catcher and various tools built into it, which he was proud to show off and pass around as we all got very high while the sun set.

7

I started wondering what I'd be like had I stayed in Corona. All my old friends were now thugs. Of course, even when I lived here I was the geek of the group. I was pretty good with my fists and got in more than my share of trouble, and I was a terrible student with the poor grades to match, but I ended up in different classes from my neighbors' when I tested my way into classes with titles like Advanced and College Prep. I figured this would have moved me away from this clique that I now couldn't imagine ever fitting in with. Then Richard and Miguel showed up. They were artists, and we had a good time talking about our favorite music and painters and doing some stoned philosophizing. These guys were smart and gentle, sensitive guys with a wonderful curiosity about the world, but as we exchanged stories it became clear that they both led violent lives as Suicidals. Being smart, being sensitive, and being creative don't necessarily save you from being a member of your community, and if that community goes to war, you'll most likely be taking your poetic ass off to war.

I looked at Dan laughing and joking as he smoked with these guys, a part of my new life in Sacramento seeming to fit okay with my old life in Corona.

Then Dan noticed that his fancy new pipe was no longer being passed around, was nowhere to be seen in fact. He asked if anyone had it and the "Nos" were defensively abrupt. Richard, Miguel, and I helped him look on the ground around where we were standing, but this was just for show. The other guys stood silently and watched us look. We all knew the pipe was in someone's pocket, and everyone knew that Dan was powerless to do anything about it.

It made me sad that I also was not going to do anything other than pretend to look for it. Not that him losing his silly pipe was such a tragedy, but it hurt to see that to his new friends, who he seemed so happy to be able to hang with, he was and would remain an outsider, and weak, worthy of no respect. They blatantly stole right in front of him, and what really stung is that I let them.

I didn't feel like hanging out anymore. I told Jamie I needed to get back to my brother's place before he put the kids to bed. The good-byes were subdued and uncomfortable. Once back at my brother's house, and out of earshot of Jamie, Dan asked me, "Did they steal my pipe?"

"Yeah, Dan, of course they did."

A few months later I was back in Corona, without Dan this time. Jamie invited me to a punk show in a storage space. I invited my brothers, James and Erick, to come along. The show was great and we were all having a good time. A few guys were trying to start a pit and I jumped in to help. The next thing I knew, someone was punching me. He wasn't great at punching. He was bad enough at it that while he was punching I was able to open up a conversation, "Woah! What's up? Why are you hitting me?"

"YOU SLAMMED INTO ME, MAN!"

"Um, yeah. This is a slam pit . . . at a punk show."

I had just made up my mind to start swinging back when I started getting hit from other directions, by people who were better at it. My brothers saw me being mobbed and jumped in. Jamie caught what was going on, and the Suicidals swarmed into the fray. One of them pulled out a gun, which he held in the air. Everyone stopped then, including the band, and someone announced that "some bitch" had called the cops. Two factions stood facing each other for a few tense seconds: the Suicidals plus three Jensen brothers on one side, and the people who I would later find out were O.C. Skins (the O.C. standing for Orange County) on the other. These skins looked Hispanic to me and they didn't have shaved heads; in fact, half of them had long hair, which confused me as to how they were "skinheads." But there was also an Orange County gang called The Nazi Lowriders, and I began to realize Southern California had its own logic that I was no longer in sync with. As sirens were heard and word spread that cops had arrived, everyone began moving toward their cars.

With a combination of alcohol and adrenaline coursing through me, I invited one of the officers to fellate me. My little brother, James, apologized to the cop and promised he was taking me home to sober up, and I got away with it, which surely had nothing to do with us being white guys.

Once in the car, Erick said with a laugh, "Well, congratulations Keith, you're a Suicidal."

"What? No I'm not."

"They all jumped in for you. If you're out somewhere and they show up and some shit goes down, and you don't jump in, they'll kill you."

"Oh."

"Yeah man, I think you don't need to go out when you come down to visit."

James laughed, "Ha! You're a Suicidal."

I was the artsy weirdo in the family, not exactly the most likely of us five brothers to end up a gang member. Hell, I was the only one of us without any tattoos.

I took Erick's advice and stuck close to his place when visiting Corona the next few times. I haven't seen Jamie again since that night.

James did see him some years later. The way I heard it, through snippets of gossip, it was when Jamie moved up to dealing and using heroin—becoming increasingly unstable and paranoid—that he ended up in prison. After he got out, James ran into him at a backyard BBQ where Jamie was grilling it up. He had his shirt off and in addition to his Suicidal tats he had prison tattoos, including a large swastika, marking his affiliation with a white supremacist gang.

James said hello, made small talk. He felt like Jamie had his head on pretty straight. He felt optimistic that Jamie would stay out of prison. Then he asked about the tats. "What's up with the white power shit?"

"That's called surviving in prison when you're a pretty, blue-eyed man," Jamie explained.

"I get it. But shouldn't you cover that up here?" James asked, looking around at the ethnically diverse crowd in the backyard waiting for burgers and dogs to be ready.

"Nah man. They know I was in. They know what's up."

And this seemed to be true, as a black man waiting on the burnt meat gave a laugh at their conversation.

Every now and then I get curious and try to track down my old friend. I check Facebook and search his name on Google. My brothers are the only people I'm still in touch with who knew him, and they haven't heard word of him since the BBQ. I imagine our lifestyles continue to diverge.

Am I a Suicidal? I go out now when I visit Southern California with no problem. I've even been to punk shows, but I didn't recognize anybody there, and nobody there recognized me. Maybe sometime before I die I'll get a "Suicidal" tattoo somewhere on my body that stays hidden by clothes, and I'll tell no one. After all, I earned that shit. I proved I was down.

I'm Suicidal.

SKINHEAD MOONSTOMPIN' WITH MONTY NEYSMITH

Nazi skinheads are a joke.

From their shaved heads to their Doc Martens boots, their entire look was stolen from one of the first truly multiracial, multicultural youth movements in England. The original skinheads were a small number of reggae- and soul-loving Jamaican immigrants and a larger number of white English kids who hung out with Jamaican immigrants and dug their music and clothes. And yes, when I say Jamaican immigrants, I mean black people! From Jamaica!

Years later, the National Front, a British fascist political party, courted the working-class skinheads, and the oxymoron that is the white-power skinhead was born. The boots, the jeans, the braces, the shaved heads: racist skinheads didn't come up with anything on their own. What's next, white-power rap? Oh damn, just Googled it, and it's a thing.

When the racist skinheads realized they looked ridiculous skanking to black music, they tried to take over the working-class

Oi genre. The great Oi punk band Sham 69 broke up because Nazi skins wanted to be their fans. It seems the love was unrequited. Their favorite band at the time said, "No thanks," and quit playing rather than accept such a shit audience.

So should you be in a position where a racist skinhead is intimidating you, standing there in their tough uniform, just remember that they're espousing white nationalism while dressed like a 1960s reggae enthusiast from London. They may as well be inviting you to enjoy some white-power yoga. Downward facing dog to upright goose step, breathe deep, and Sieg Heil the rising sun.

This proves to be hugely confusing to anyone outside of the punk scene and/or under the age of thirty, but there are still non-racist skinheads, as there have been from the beginning. SHARPS (Skinheads Against Racial Prejudice), Trojan Skinheads, Trads, and others continue to enjoy reggae, soul, ska, Oi, and punk rock, skanking in their Doc Martens and braces and embracing diversity in all its danceable glory.

While researching the roots of skinhead culture, I stumbled across a gem, the 1969 song "Skinhead Moonstomp" by the band Symarip, an all-black reggae band who also recorded "Skinhead Girl," "Skinhead Jamboree," and a rockin' version of "These Boots Were Made for Walking," with "walking" replaced by "stomping." They were, it turns out, the first group to record and release tunes specifically geared toward the skinhead movement. I looked up band members online and in short order found myself on the phone with keyboardist and songwriter Monty Neysmith.

"Irie," he answered the phone, in a heavy Caribbean accent. Neysmith coached me on spelling his band's name and provided a list of other monikers they performed under, as they often changed their name to get out of contracts. "Symarip" came from their earlier name, The Pyramids, spelled backward and altered slightly.

Monty then told me the story of how Symarip came to be the first skinhead band. The band was touring Europe as Prince Buster's backing band, as their single "Train Tour to Rainbow City" was making a mark on the charts. Then Graeme Goodall from Doctor Bird (a reggae record label) came to the band with a track by another reggae artist, Derrick Morgan. "Graeme says, 'This is a good riddim, why don't you guys write a song to it?'" Another member of the band, observing that skinheads had been coming out to their shows in increasing numbers, suggested they write a song for them.

The response was immediate, to say the least. "We recorded the song on Monday. And Friday, the same week. We recorded and then released it in two days." They didn't think much of it, and they made their way to a gig, stopping at a favorite record shop in Shepherd's Bush (West London). As they approached the store, they noticed a long line running out the store and down the sidewalk. "We didn't know at the time what they were buying but when we passed by the kids everybody started shouting, 'Skinhead Moon Stomp.' We thought, 'How could these people know that song already, we just recorded it?'"

Capitalizing on the success of this first single, the album *Skinhead Moonstomp* soon followed with additional tracks ripe for skanking. Monty loved the skinheads they'd now secured as a loyal and passionate fan base: "It was a great movement, because it was all mostly working-class people. Weekends, putting on their braces and their boots or the other half putting on their suits, and looking slick and going out and having fun and, most importantly of all, they loved Jamaican music, so we couldn't help but loving them."

While most people, including myself, picture a club full of skinheads and imagine a rough night ahead, it wasn't the case for Symarip in the late sixties and early seventies. "Whenever we went to a place, I would look in the audience from backstage. And the saying is, if you saw one skinhead in the audience it was gonna be a great night. That's how we felt about the skinheads."

Growing up around violent racist skins, and other skins who were far preferable to the Nazi variety but who also seemed mostly defined by violence, this was hard to imagine. To Monty's recollections, around 5 percent of the skinheads at that time were black. He said, "Not many," but this seems like a lot to me compared to the skinhead scene in the states, where I think I've witnessed three black skinheads in person, ever. I asked if there were many women. And while he remembered the men outnumbering the women in the scene, there were still plenty of skinhead girls to be found.

"Well, there was one I saw, I fell in love with her and that's why I wrote that song." I'm delighted to hear that "Skinhead Girl" was about a specific skinhead girl. "She became my girlfriend after a while." Monty laughs. "She couldn't help it, writing a song for her."

Monty described a vibrant scene and told me it was not a particularly tough one plagued by fighting. He doesn't recall a single show where violence was an issue.

And were there overtly racist skinheads at the time, in the early seventies? If there were, Monty didn't come across them, but he managed never to experience them later in the eighties' two-tone scene either and in fact somehow hasn't been bothered by them to this day.

"Never had run-ins with the racist ones and none of them came to our show that I know of. If they came they were quiet in a corner or something. We never had any confrontations with them."

Monty Neysmith continues to tour and to play reggae music today, touring out from his home base in Atlanta, Georgia. He left Symarip when they got too comfortable for his liking, playing the hits to vacationers at ski lodges. His heart is with reggae, and his heart is still with skinheads. Hearing him speak of their scene with such affection, I wonder what it felt like to hear that racists had somehow managed to make "skinhead" synonymous with racism and nationalism.

Monty has to explain the real roots of skinhead culture constantly, a lifelong ambassador for the scene. "In America, they think all skinheads are racists and nationalists and horrible people, you know, and I try to explain to them that these people stole the culture from the real skinheads what formed in England. I been trying to educate people on that and explain to them that real skinheads love Jamaica, love Jamaican food, love Jamaican music, love the way we talk. They love everything about Jamaica. And they come out and they support Jamaican music, don't care where it is. They're the ones that keep Jamaican music alive through all these bad times."

Is a Monty Neysmith show likely to be attended by skinheads today? Absolutely. "I just did a tour in America here, and we have skinheads show up all over. We did a show in Detroit and skinheads came over from Canada, across the border. They love it, I can tell you that."

And he still treats them to "Skinhead Moonstomp" at every show he plays, bringing the skinhead men up on stage to dance during the song, and then having the women take their place for "Skinhead Girl."

After talking to me about the white nationalists making so

much noise in America and around the world today, Monty reminded me that it's nothing new. He told of a delightful response by Symarip and reggae star Millie Small ("My Boy Lollipop") in the seventies when racist politician Enoch Powell warned of the dangers of allowing brown-skinned immigrants into England. They recorded a song titled "Enoch Powell." The song is a rocker, describing proud, hardworking, brown-skinned English men and women working all week, and dedicating their weekends to dancing to reggae music. She doesn't attack Powell directly, or even mention him beyond singing his name repeatedly in the chorus. What a great image, immigrants from the West Indies, and skinheads, skanking together in sweaty dance halls to the name of this hateful, silly man who would be so confused by it all.

I arrived from Kingston Town
And now live at the bullring
Got to go to Wolverhampton
Help my brothers do a thing
They work all week
To keep the British country running
Weekend it's reggae time
And the neighbours find it funny
So we all sing
Enoch, Enoch, Enoch Powell, Lord, Lord
Enoch, Enoch, Enoch Powell
Enoch, Enoch, Enoch Powell, Lord, Lord
Enoch, Enoch, Enoch Powell

The kids all stomp their boots so much
The dance floor's really shaking
They're having fun then going Dutch

I feel my poor heart aching, so we all sing
Enoch, Enoch, Enoch Powell, Lord, Lord
Enoch, Enoch, Enoch Powell
Enoch, Enoch, Enoch Powell, Lord, Lord
Enoch, Enoch, Enoch Powell
One day there'll come a time
When all men will be brothers
They'll talk as well as dance
And live and love with each other
And they'll all sing
Enoch, Enoch, Enoch Powell, Lord, Lord
Enoch, Enoch, Enoch Powell
Enoch, Enoch, Enoch Powell
Enoch, Enoch, Enoch Powell

"If you are really concerned about Nazis' safety think about it like this—if more of them had been punched in the thirties maybe we wouldn't have had to kill so many of them in the forties."
                    —Chris Cubas, Comedian

PUNCHING NAZIS

Full disclosure: I've never punched a Nazi.

This is my great shame.

My uncle Joe fought Nazis and had the tattoos to prove it. Back then, tattoos were for war vets and convicts. His tats involved eagles and snakes and American flags and initials that I didn't understand. When I asked my mom about them, she explained that Uncle Joe had fought in World War II, as if this was explanation enough, an obvious reason for him being a tatted-up old dude. I wasn't sure of the connection between fighting in WWII and having tattoos, but I accepted it. Recently my dad informed me that dear old Uncle Joe had served with the heroic Audie Murphy's company. He fought alongside the author and star of *To Hell and Back*. He'd earned his ink.

Uncle Joe never talked to me about his time at war, but I'm pretty sure he punched some Nazis, unlike his no-good, shiftless nephew, who has never punched a Nazi, not one single Nazi.

And it isn't just a matter of timing, I'm loath to admit. I've had opportunities. I have been in the presence of plenty of latter-day Nazis.

My friend and noted podcaster, Carrie Poppy, witnessed me in one of my favorite activities of late, fighting with liberals who think we should respect the free speech of Nazis. She proposed that most of the people discussing the issue of whether to punch, or even support the punching of, Nazis had never met, and likely would never meet, a Nazi—or any white supremacist for that matter.

I think she couldn't be more wrong. We see and interact with white supremacists every day, and it's our privilege not to notice them.

Recently I took my daughter to a Science Fiction Con, for a little father-daughter geek-out session. A man was openly, freely walkin' about with a swastika tattoo on his chest. He wore a tank top, seemingly to make sure his hate showed. I noticed it, but the people around me did not seem to. Darth Vader was happy to pose for a picture with him, which may be a case of really sticking to one's character, but it disturbed me, and where was the Captain America cosplayer when we need him to give one of his infamous star-spangled Nazi face punches?

With my seven-year-old with me, I wasn't comfortable engaging him. When I mentioned it later to one of the organizers of the Con, the first question she asked me was "Was he causing trouble, saying stuff, showing it off, anything like that? Or just minding his own business but with a tattoo on his arm?"

I answered, "YES! He was causing trouble. He was walking around with a swastika tattoo on display." He was openly, proudly claiming association with a group that killed six million Jews! He was erasing all doubt, and letting us know that he himself claims membership in a group that, the last time they were allowed to get too strong, resulted in the deaths of sixty million people before they could be stopped.

Then my fellow liberals lined up to recite the same questions I get every time this subject comes up: "What about free speech?"

This was a private event! No shirt, no shoes, no service. Swastika on clear display, no fucking service. You wouldn't let someone sit and verbally harass your other patrons with hateful speech; why is it any different when they write it on their bodies, and let their tattoos do the talking?

Well, how do you know he hasn't changed and just hasn't had a chance to cover up the tattoo yet?
The tattoo was on his chest. He wore a tank top to keep it visible. If someone has changed their stripes, why would they go out with such a hurtful, hateful symbol on display? I'm sorry, but if you're not putting a Band-Aid over it, wearing a scarf, keeping your long sleeves on, then you still don't care enough about the comfort of Jewish people, people of color, gay people, or disabled people. All this blowback and I didn't even mention that someone should have punched him in his face. I was just expressing my disappointment that I, or someone else, hadn't engaged him, that the organizers hadn't asked him to cover it up. What wonderful people we are, pat on the back, wanting to protect the rights and feelings of this Nazi.

Would I have punched him? Maybe. Probably not, but maybe, if I had a clean shot and could do it without too much risk to myself. What I would have liked to have done is just ask him why he was displaying a swastika, maybe on a livestream video. I would have loved to have pestered him about it until he left, or struck me and put himself in jail, and I would have liked it if the organizers told him to leave, or to at least cover it up, and if the cosplayers said "no, thank you" to posing with him and his swastika, and if this geek community, already horribly lacking in diversity, would have done anything to show they gave two shits about the comfort of their guests who weren't as lily-white as they were. I adore the utopian, egalitarian vision of *Star Trek*. I dig seeing it cosplayed, but I'd love to see it actually applied even more.

And yes, I also would have liked to have given him a good Shatner right cross across the jaw. I'd only have Shatnered him if I could have made it a sucker Shatner. I'm willing to get my ass kicked by a Nazi if it means they go to jail. I'm only willing to hit first if I can get away with it. Fight fair? No. I don't care about treating Nazis fairly. I couldn't have won a fight with this big bull of a man, which I'm sure had something to do with his willingness to have that tattoo showing. No point getting beat up and getting arrested for assault. I'm all for punching Nazis, but punch smart. Punch to win.

Even though I'm sure I made the right choice, I still was bummed to not have gotten my shot at punching a Nazi. There should be a service where you can sponsor someone punching a Nazi. You'd get a picture of your Nazi to put on your refrigerator so you could tell your friends, "Yep that's my Nazi, got punched real good and for less than the price of a cup of coffee a week!" Maybe Sally Struthers could speak over background music by Sarah McLachlan as images scroll by of sad, unpunched Nazis, needing your sponsorship so they can get the punching they so deserve.

Back to my friend Carrie. Yeah, we meet Nazis all the time, and they're not usually so brazen about it. They've taken to using code words like "alt-right," or "racial realist." They're holding "Free speech rallies" and they're celebrating Trump's win (even Sieg Heiling their leader, alt-right poster boy Richard Spencer, when they don't realize they're on camera), and they're out with torches mourning the removal of statues of their Confederate heroes in New Orleans, or the removal of their traitorous, hateful flag in South Carolina.

White nationalism is on the rise again and now has more open and blatant influence in Washington. We've seen the result of waiting too long to oppose it, and so have the white nationalists who would like to meet and organize openly and gain power while being "civil" for as long as possible.

The discussion on whether to punch Nazis kicked into high gear on January 20, 2017. I was in Austin, Texas, for some shows, staying with friends of mine who would probably rather I keep their names out of this.

I love Austin, as I love any liberal town surrounded by the reddest of red states, but the visit wasn't all vegan BBQ and prank-calling gun shops ("Do you carry clay pigeons for target practice? You do? That is SO great. Thank you! Thank you for carrying a vegan option. You're open on Ramadan, yeah?"), for this was the day of Donald J. Trump's inconceivable inauguration as President of the United States of America.

The alt-right Nazis knew this was a victory for their side even as many of my fellow liberals tried not to see it as such. Steve Bannon, who helped popularize "alt-right" as a phrase and movement while editor of Breitbart News Network, wrote Herr Trump's apocalyptic, Frank Miller-esque inaugural speech and joined the administration as Trump's chief strategist. A video of the National Policy Institute, which bills itself as "an independent organization dedicated to the heritage, identity, and future of people of European descent in the United States, and around the world," celebrating Trump's win at their annual meeting, had been heavily circulating. The money shot of this clip was Richard Spencer taking the stage, opening with "Hail Trump, hail our people, hail victory!" and going on to spout anti-Semitism and even throw around some of Adolf's favorite phrases, such as *Lügenpresse*—"lying press"—as the crowd Sieg Heiled him.

My heart was heavy, my brain busy, and then came some much-needed comic relief as Richard Spencer was punched in the face on camera while being interviewed about his racist Pepe the Frog lapel pin. Some brave soul had finally taken the initiative to say, clearly, "No! You don't get to just stand out in the open in America as your band of neo-Nazis rise in power." I laughed. I cheered. I even teared up a bit at the beauty of it.

And immediately I got into heated arguments with other liberals about whether it's right and good to punch Nazis.

Well, you call anyone a Nazi who disagrees with your ideology.
Well, yeah, if by my ideology you mean that straight, able-bodied, cisgendered, Christian, white males aren't superior to the rest of us.

Punching Richard Spencer gives him more attention.
His publicity trajectory was up and up before he got punched. He was IN FRONT of cameras when he was punched. He was punched out of the frame, not into the frame. You'd never heard of him before that? I did. You should be ashamed. You weren't paying enough attention. Glad you've heard of him now so you'll recognize him if you see him on the street, and can punch him in the face.

Ignoring fascism has repeatedly failed. Ignoring the threat of white supremacist fascists is what brought us to this place to begin with.

Aren't you worried about people using this as an excuse to punch anyone they want to punch and justifying it by calling that person a Nazi?

Sure. That's a reasonable concern, but I'm more afraid of people using that concern to condemn punching legit Nazis, because that's a thing I actually see happening.

But you're convicting them of a thought crime. If they're not doing anything wrong, they should be allowed to think and express thoughts, even those you find abhorrent. If they didn't strike first, it's assault.

They asked to be associated with genocide, with large-scale murder, with setting into motion a war that was the deadliest in the history of humanity, taking sixty million lives. I'm only taking them at their word. If they volunteer to associate themselves with and champion these crimes, a punch in the face is the least they deserve.

The same goes for the Confederate flag. You want to associate yourself with enslaving black people and terrorizing them after the Civil War? You can have a punch in the face too if you think for a minute that you should be able to go out in public with that shit and be treated with any level of civility.

What is it with these goons wanting to fly the flags of history's biggest losers anyway? And what is it with "real Americans" claiming patriotism while flying the flag of that time they fought so hard not to be America, or the flag of America's greatest historical foe?

Never again. That's supposed to be the lesson of WWII and of the Holocaust, yeah? Waiting until they strike first isn't *never again.* It's *again.*

When we call the alt-right "Nazis," it's not that feared "slippery slope" of calling anyone a Nazi so we can oppose them. It's SUCH an obvious dog whistle. If you fall for it, they're making a joke of you. They are Sieg Heiling! They are spouting anti-Semitism! They are calling for a white homeland! They're doing cute things like peppering their speeches with phrases that Adolf Hitler popularized, and they're saying them IN GERMAN! Can it even be called a dog whistle at that point? It's a funny haircut goose-stepping with a megaphone at that point, isn't it?

You're taking them too seriously. Giving them too much credit. They are a tiny minority with no power.
Um . . . Steve Bannon is, er, *was* in the White House and still wields influence with the president! At what point do you take them seriously? Have we forgotten that Hitler and his brown shirts were once just street thugs? This sounds too much like, "Oh, stop fretting. Trump isn't a serious candidate. Trump will be one of the first to drop out. Trump will never be the Republican nominee. Trump can't possibly win the presidency."

They repeatedly use the camouflage of jokes and irony to recruit and organize right under our noses. "Pepe the Frog is JUST a cartoon. We're just trolling for LOLs. Get a sense of humor. We're championing free speech by pushing its limits. We just like to see you cry."

Convincing us that they're joking is their best trick, and we keep falling for it. Gavin McInnes, founder of the self-described "far right men's group" The Proud Boys, says he will sue anyone who calls his band of racist hipsters racist. He also told the *New York Times*, "I love being white and I think it's something to be proud of, I don't want our culture diluted." But don't worry, he was just kidding. He was quoted by Gawker as saying the statement was only meant to goad easily offended liberals. Ha ha, I get it! This guy is hilarious!

I have always assumed that a percentage of trolls in the alt-right ranks are indeed just young and enjoy the thrill of pissing off the world by playing with sacred cows, getting a reaction so easily, and that many of them will grow out of it as they get the gravity of what they're playing with and see some of the hurt that has made these symbols and ideas so charged and so dangerous. But when the big conflicts happen, when there is doxing of and death threats aimed at feminists or other civil rights activists, when things get especially nasty, as in Gamergate, too few defected. Too few said, "Oh, no, this isn't what I wanted. This is too much." And far too many doubled down. If anything their numbers seemed to swell, or at the very least their volume increased to a deafening roar.

What's the worst-case scenario here? If they are kidding, just pranking us all, and we fall for it and beat them down, then their prank worked, right? If they're bloody and bowed, they can say with pride, "Ha! Fooled ya!" I tell ya, I for one will be so embarrassed and will gladly offer up a "You got me! Good one."

Aren't you giving these hateful people too much of your time and energy?

Whenever someone says this to me I imagine them saying it to my uncle Joe when he was spending literally ALL his time and energy fighting fascists in Europe. I don't give hateful assholes enough of my time. I ain't doing shit to earn a tattoo like the ones that adorned Uncle Joe's skin.

I like to consider myself a positive person, and also a peaceful person. I try to put out some positive, peaceful energy in between going off about Nazis in need of punching. My social media posts are:

- Picture my kid drew
- Funny cartoon
- Invitation to come see me perform stand-up
- Imploring you to punch Nazis, or at least stop condemning people who are punching Nazis
- Another picture my kid drew

And honestly, while I might be cheering on antifascist violence, I do so pretty, well, cheerfully. Why do we always focus on the negative? When sports fans cheer their team winning, we don't accuse them of being negative about the team who lost. They cheer on the Golden State Warriors. I cheer on the Golden State Nazi Punchers.

We are so divided!
Good!
 I don't want to be united with assholes.

But Martin Luther King said . . .
Okay, stop. At the risk of joining the throngs of white people cherry-picking MLK quotes to support their own viewpoint, he also said:

But it is not enough for me to stand before you tonight and condemn riots. It would be morally irresponsible for me to do that without, at the same time, condemning the contingent, intolerable conditions that exist in our society. These conditions are the things that cause individuals to feel that they have no other alternative than to engage in violent rebellions to get attention. And I must say tonight that a riot is the language of the unheard. And what is it America has failed to hear? . . . It has failed to hear that the promises of freedom and justice have not been met. And it has failed to hear that large segments of white society are more concerned about tranquility and the status quo than about justice and humanity.

Yes!

He also said:

First, I must confess that over the past few years I have been gravely disappointed with the white moderate. I have almost reached the regrettable conclusion that the Negro's great stumbling block in his stride toward freedom is not the White Citizens' Council or the Ku Klux Klanner, but the white moderate, who is more devoted to "order" than to justice; who prefers a negative peace which is the absence of tension to a positive peace which is the presence of justice; who constantly says: "I agree with you in the goal you seek, but I cannot agree with your methods of direct action."

Unless you're a scholar when it comes to the complex and nuanced views of the good Reverend—I'm not—maybe be careful about quoting him to support your argument.

And while we're at it, Gandhi, a veteran, was a brilliant military tactician who managed to beat the British Army in the only way possible. This ain't that. This is a different situation.

India achieved its independence with these tactics of passive resistance. King tried the same approach here, made some important progress, but over four decades later I don't think you can fault people for wanting to try a different strategy.

But when Antifa shows up to a protest it's disrespecting the people who organized the nonviolent event.

That's true, if the event is a march or demonstration with an arbitrary date and location. But if you're talking about a protest on a campus where Spencer is speaking, sorry, the peaceful protestors don't own that space, they didn't create that event; Spencer did. Go be peaceful against Spencer at another location.

So you think it should be legal for private citizens to punch people?

Nope.

I think private citizens should be sometimes willing to go to jail for something they believe in.

So you're okay with rioting, too?

Yes, sometimes, when it doesn't involve your favorite sports team losing, or winning, and so is everyone who has ever championed the Boston Tea Party or the Stonewall Riots.

When you suffer under systematic oppression, who could blame you for not being so concerned with society's rules?

Civilization doesn't mean much to you when you're hungry. You will steal, cheat, do what you have to do to eat. Civilization depends on not allowing a large segment of the population to starve. Who could expect someone to sit and starve to death as part of their civic duty? So why would we expect someone to be "civil" as the forces that have resulted in the worst violence in human history start to reorganize and gain strength?

Let me explain what should be obvious. I'm not suggesting you should get up right now, find a racist, and punch them in the face. If you did so, I'd totally get it. I'd empathize with you. But let's be real, what this conversation is really about is punching Richard Spencer, who is actively seeking to cause harm. It's about stopping white supremacists from speaking at our colleges, claiming our public spaces as safe zones for promoting a historically deadly and disastrous agenda. You have another way to fight their rise to power, great. But I can't look at the people who have, throughout history, been the victims of white power and tell them how to fight it, or tell them they have to be "civil" because the people who hold the most ethnic privilege and power are being "civil" in their efforts to reclaim America for themselves, to continue the oppression of nonwhites, and to otherwise cling to power. And I won't criticize the white people who are willing to use their privilege, and their bodies, fists, etc., to stand against the white-power movers and shakers.

Do-good liberals who like to cherry-pick Martin Luther King Jr. quotes also love to point out blues musician Daryl Davis, subject of the documentary film *Accidental Courtesy*, as someone who is "doing it right." Davis, a black man, engages members of the KKK and has convinced quite a few of them to not only leave the Klan, but to give him their robes as a trophy for the good guys. Look, I love this. I think it's great. My hero, Louis Armstrong, could play the trumpet so beautifully, he literally played the racism out of at least one man's heart according to Charles L. Black Jr., who, at sixteen years old, was so moved when he heard Armstrong play in Austin, Texas, in 1931 that he had to abandon the racism he'd been raised with. Black would go on to help Thurgood Marshall write the legal brief for Linda Brown in the historic *Brown v. Board of Education* case. Do you have that talent? If so, go use it. Go convert some racists. But don't sit, feeling lovely about yourself with your handful of formerly racists pals, as the unconverted gain direct influence into the White House (again)

33

and are emboldened to start marching in the streets and holding rallies at our state capitols (again). Don't look down on those who are standing in their way.

Nazi punchers, I for one salute you and thank you for your service.

THE VIOLENT FEMMES

I was sixteen years old when I learned firsthand that it's not easy to fall asleep in a parking lot with a cement block for a pillow and bright incandescent lightbulbs keeping out the dark. We could have found a darker parking lot, I'm sure, but then it would've been harder to sleep for reasons of fear rather than petty annoyance. This parking lot would do.

We'd come to San Francisco, my friend Ryan and I, with our friend Ben and his girlfriend of the week, Sheryl, to see one of our favorite bands, the Violent Femmes, play The Warfield.

Sheryl's constant complaining, and Ben's kowtowing to her presence, had me eager to ditch the two of them, so after the concert Ryan and I left with two cute girls who'd invited us back to their place.

We left the concert with our new friends and were in line at Burger King when a homeless man wearing infinite layers of clothing, creating the illusion of immense size, pushed his way to the front of the line.

"Give me some water," he demanded, slamming his cup down on the counter. "I'm Mr. A! Don't touch me! I'm dirty!"

As evidence to his proclaimed dirtiness, he used the corner of the counter to squeegee his palms, leaving a puddle of what looked like Crisco behind. I realized he was coated, every inch of him, clothing and all, in this thick, white grease. For two suburban teens on an adventure in the city, this was intoxicatingly urban.

After getting our burgers and fries we followed our dates onto the BART train toward Richmond. I scored some smooches as we sped through the night. Ryan didn't do as well, as he never stopped talking long enough to make a move or be moved on. The train stopped and the girls said good-night.

"Good-night? Aren't we going with you?" I asked.

"No! We have to call my mom to come pick us up."

"Well, what the hell are we supposed to do?"

This was not, we were informed, their problem. The two girls disappeared into a minivan, leaving behind the lingering taste of fast-food kisses and phone numbers scribbled on a BK napkin.

We found a Denny's, figuring we'd spend the night there, but sitting at the bar drinking really bad coffee under the hateful glare of a tweeker waitress got old quick.

Ryan applied for a job. In his flannel shirt, plaid trench coat with tears and patches, foot-long Mohawk, and combat boots, at one o'clock in the morning, Ryan applied for a job.

Then we made our way to the parking lot. My army jacket could serve as a pillow for my head or warmth for my body. I went back and forth. We were relieved when a man walked by and asked if we'd seen any cars parked in the lot.

"No, I'm pretty sure it's closed," I answered, noticing the gas can and length of hose he carried.

"We can help you find some cars, though," Ryan offered, and we hopped up and started walking alongside this stranger who

36

was sure to be more entertaining than trying to sleep in a parking lot.

"I just gotta siphon a bit of gas. I'm trying to get to Fresno and I got a damn hole in my gas tank. I siphon some gas, it gets me a few miles and I stop and siphon more gas. Hell of a way to travel. Some asshole put a hole in my goddamn gas tank. Son of a bitch." As he spoke rapidly he undid a gas cap on an old truck, slid the hose in, paused to suck up some gas, spit, coughed, and as his can filled he continued right where he'd left off. "Son of a bitch. I got a beautiful old Saab on the back of my truck. Gonna scrap it in Fresno. Then I'll have some money. God damn, I've been doing this all night. If only I could drive the fuckin' Saab. But she ain't safe on the road. Oh no."

We reached his truck and his Saab. I'm not normally much of a car person, but I do admire a few vehicles. Old Volvos, old VWs, and old Saabs.

"Why the hell are you gonna scrap this awesome car?" I asked, seeing a good-looking vehicle hiked up on the back of a truck that looked like it had only recently met with some manner of violence that transformed it into a flatbed. Leaving my question unanswered, our jittery friend drove off toward Fresno and we went back to Denny's.

We had enough money to split a side order of one pancake. We asked if we could have coffee refills, since we'd bought coffee a few hours earlier, and amazingly the waitress poured us a couple of mugs. She was really nice this time around. Maybe we'd gone, in her eyes, from being two annoying kids out late after a show to two homeless kids who couldn't actually help being annoying. We tried not to be pains in her ass, which I think she appreciated.

I figured it was late enough in the morning to call the two girls who'd gotten us in this mess to begin with. From the pay phone outside I called them collect, since we'd spent the last of our change on a pancake.

"Oh my God, do you know how early it is?"

"I sure do. Nothing like sleeping in a parking lot to let you know just how early it is."

"Oh my God, you slept in a parking lot? I'm so sorry."

"Hey, can we come over?"

"My parents will be gone in an hour, come over then."

We got directions and slowly made our way toward an idyllic suburban neighborhood full of big cars and big homes. We found the right house and were greeted by two girls who looked much younger in daylight, especially when surrounded by a mess of siblings and friends of siblings. I recognized this house. This was the house in every neighborhood with mostly absent parents and lots of girls hanging out all the time. I loved this house.

We were no longer interested in kisses, but we felt they owed us money and food and, what's that? Would we like some wine coolers? Why, sure.

"Won't your parents notice all the wine coolers missing?" Ryan asked.

"No. My mom is an idiot. She buys them for our school lunches. She doesn't realize that they have alcohol in them."

They were anxious to give us anything we wanted if we'd just leave. While the daylight and squeaky-clean environment served to make them look more youthful, I'm sure we looked worse, dirtier, and, to our delight, much more punk rock.

Their father was a gynecologist. Of course he was. It was too perfect. We left the house full of cute rich girls, realizing that if we came back in two years it would be heaven on earth, but for now it was mostly annoying. Our bellies were full of sliced deli meat sandwiches made on French bread, and real fruit Popsicles.

We had a few bucks now so we caught the BART train toward Oakland, where Ryan's brother hung out at a guy named Screamer's house. Ryan thought he remembered where Screamer lived but we ended up lost, wandering around Oakland until we ran into a local punk who went by the name Phlegm.

"Hey, little, whiny shits, what are you doing here?" he greeted us.

"Looking for my brother," Ryan answered.

"He ain't here, dude."

"Well, is Screamer's place near here?"

"Yeah, you stupid shit. It's one block up that way. See you little shits later, I'm going to work."

We found Screamer's place, which was a converted garage behind his mom's house. It was filthy. One futon faced a TV that never went off. A scum-coated bathroom was the only other room.

Screamer's girlfriend worked, while Screamer and a rotating cast of punks hung out in front of the TV all day drinking and doing whatever drugs were available. Screamer was happy to see us.

"Hey, fuckers! Dude, your brother's coming to town today!"

This was great news. Jason was coming into town, most likely to score some drugs, and we could then get a ride back to Sacramento with him. I used Screamer's phone to call my mom, who thought I was a few blocks away at Ben's house and was pretty pissed to find out I was still in the Bay Area. I told her we'd be home the next day and that unless she wanted to come get us there was nothing I could do about it.

We passed the next few hours watching Black Entertainment Television while Screamer shouted all kinds of racist shit at the screen. "Ha ha! Another chicken commercial. Goddamn, how can you say them [n-words] don't love chicken when every other fuckin' ad is for fried chicken ON THEIR CHANNEL?!"

Ryan and I found a corner to sit and talk and we tried to stay out of Screamer and company's way. Then Phlegm showed up again.

"Oh fuck, these little shits are here? You sniveling cunts should go home. Who the fuck wants little brats around? This ain't a fuckin' day care." He was especially proud of the day care line. It would be repeated incessantly for the duration of our visit. I ignored him but Ryan couldn't resist a fight.

"Why are you talking in a British accent? You're not British."

"Fuck you!"

"And you look pretty pathetic picking on the two youngest guys in the room. It shows that you're on the bottom of the pecking order around here, just desperate to put someone beneath you." Ryan, who was the scrawniest person I knew, loved to run his mouth, seemingly had no fear of getting his ass kicked, and somehow usually managed to come out unscathed.

Phlegm responded predictably, "I'm going to kick your fucking ass."

As Phlegm walked toward Ryan, I gave him a quick reminder. "Dude, you might want to remember that he's Jason's brother, and Jason's on his way here." I followed by giving him a way out. "Hey, I thought you were going to work."

"Oh yeah, shit, work!" Phlegm became very excited now. "My boss cut off his fucking thumb. I couldn't fucking believe it. He cut it all the way off. I picked it up and handed it to him. He told me to take the day off and he drove off in his car with his fucking thumb in his lunch box. IN HIS FUCKING LUNCH BOX! It was so crazy."

Phlegm forgot about Ryan and joined the other punks spewing racist hate at the BET. Not calling them out on their racism made me feel like a real chump, but I decided I just needed to get through the day and get back home. Just as the n-word comments were reaching a fever pitch, the door opened and a huge black man in white Doc Martens boots with black laces and a Malcolm X t-shirt stood in the doorway.

Screamer jumped to his feet and I prepared to run as they walked toward each other. My heart pounded rapidly in my chest. Then they gave each other a bear hug. They went into the bathroom together to do some buying and selling and then the guy actually sat in front of the TV for a spell to join the rest in laughing at the "crazy [n-words]." We'd found a strange world.

Jason showed up soon after and Ryan and I begged him to take us to get something to eat. He said he'd take us on a run in an hour. I wasn't sure what a run was, but it seemed to involve eating and that was a good thing.

Sixty minutes later we went out to the recycling place to empty Jason's car of many bags full of cans and bottles. He got a few bucks for this and then we went to a taco spot where I had the best food I'd ever eaten in my life. Then came "the run." We rolled up to the recycling plant, now closed, and parked in the alley. Jason instructed Ryan to wait with the car and had me follow him. A couple large sheets of cardboard over the barbed wire made clearing the fence a breeze. We hurled full bags of cans over the fence and Ryan loaded them into the station wagon. Once the car was full we crowded in with the bags and sped off.

We stopped at a 7-11 to stockpile Home Run Pies, Twinkies, Cokes, and other essentials to get us through the night. Back at Screamer's I called my mom again and told her I would have to spend at least one more night in The Bay. She wasn't too happy, but when I told her we were with Ryan's brother she felt better. If she'd really known Jason, she would have jumped in her minivan right that second and come after me.

Then it was time to smoke crack.

Screamer's girlfriend, that's the only name she was given as far as I knew, had come home from work and the punks circled up to smoke. Ryan and I retreated to our corner. Just as the lighter flicked on and flame was touched to crack, a small speaker next to the door crackled to life.

"Craig, what are you doin' in there? Craig?" It was Screamer's (a.k.a. Craig's) mom. Craig was such a pedestrian name for this legendary scum punk. He hollered back, "Nothing, Mom. Leave me alone." And suddenly he looked more like a little boy playing dress-up than the threatening monster I'd come to think of him as. He took a hit and then stood up.

The following dance was so well choreographed, Ryan and I could scarcely trust our eyes. Screamer's girlfriend took the pipe and turned her back to the front window just as an old lady's face appeared in it howling, "Craig!" She took her hit and Screamer slammed the blinds shut. The pipe was passed to Phlegm, whose back was to the side window, just in time to hide it from the old lady as she appeared in this window seconds before Screamer slammed more blinds shut. "Craig? What are you doing, Craig?" The pipe made its way to Jason, hiding it from a third window behind him, and the whole routine repeated. "Crrrraaaiiiggg!" It was crack cocaine slapstick. Ryan and I fell over laughing. Then we ate some Twinkies and drank some Cokes and joined the circle, now that the crack had been put away.

We talked about the girls who had lured us out here. Screamer thought we should go back to their place in the morning and shake them down for more money. Ryan and I actually started to find our place in this insane little scene and we enjoyed swapping jokes and stories, though we had to struggle to ignore Phlegm's constant references to day care.

Eventually Screamer and his girl went to sleep on the futon. Jason had the mattress that was lying in one corner, and Ryan and I grabbed some floor. We both woke up early the next morning, anxious to get out of there. It tried our patience having to wait for Jason to wake up.

Neither of us was capable of being quiet, and Screamer would yell at us every time we started talking until finally Jason got sick of the noise, got up, and we left for Sacramento at last.

Jason stopped on the way out of town to sell the cans and bottles back to the place we'd stolen them from the night before.

Ryan and I spent the last of our money at Denny's, this time having a full breakfast that felt like a feast. Jason was angry that we neither bought him breakfast nor paid for gas, but we pointed out that we hadn't gotten a cut of the recycling money, either. He gave us each a hard punch in the arm.

It was great to get home, have a shower, brush my teeth, put on clean clothes, and eat real food. Ryan and I worked on exaggerating what a good time we'd had so that Ben would feel like an ass for choosing his latest girlfriend over his friends.

The Violent Femmes were fantastic. Quite a show.

"Nazis hate leftists because they think we're being phony. Leftists hate Nazis because we know they're being authentic."
   —Cate Gary, Comedian/Trumpslayer

SACRAMENTO, CALIFORNIA: HOME OF THE NAZI PUNCHERS

I live in Sacramento, the capitol city of California, and we've had our share of Nazis in need of face punching. Most recently, the Traditionalist Worker Party attempted to hold a rally at the capitol building, with support from their buddies, the Golden State Skinheads. They were met by protesters, many associating themselves with the Antifa (antifascist) movement, and violence ensued.

Several police officers, who seemed to mostly just stand by and watch the melee, were quoted in the papers as saying it was not the "permit holders" who initiated the violence. The clumsy and robotic phrase "permit holders" is how far the police will go to avoid calling them white supremacists, skinheads, or Nazis, all things these groups call themselves. The other side started it? They somehow missed the opening blows of this fight, I guess, where white supremacists enslaved black people, burned crosses in fields, hung black people from trees, made a strong effort at wiping Jewish people from the face of the earth, along with the disabled and homosexuals, and caused the bloodiest conflicts this world has ever seen. It's worth noting that a sweet little Nazi skinhead did all the stabbing that day.

Why did Sacramento respond so strongly?

Maybe because in the eighties and early nineties our downtown became a war zone as SHARPS (Skinheads Against Racial Prejudice) and others started fighting back against white-power skinheads who had taken over our music scene.

The danger in ignoring Nazis is that they don't give up ground easily. Once they'd made a Nazi safe space of Sacramento's streets, trying to push them out saw them escalating. There were shots fired, at least one fatal stabbing, a local music promoter put in the hospital with a broken back.

A group of scooter enthusiasts called the Burgundy Tops may have seemed an easy target for our local skinheads when they were spotted hanging out by Tower Theater, but the Tops instead delivered a thorough beatdown to the bald bullies outside of a local café. If this rumble had taken place a decade later, it would have been filmed from multiple angles and posted on Youtube. This fact brings a tear to my eyes. How cool would it be to see members of the best-dressed scene in town beating up a bunch of Nazi skinheads outside of a classic movie theater?! Ron Howard, call me.

Eventually, enough of the Nazi boneheads either grew up enough to move on or went to prison and lost their grip on our town. They're still here, for sure. A few years back a group of them all got out of prison around the same time and reunited with their buddies on the outside, and it was like old times again for a week or two. On the night when a local band got their asses kicked after a show, mostly just for being poor examples of proud, masculine, white men, I was sitting with my own bandmates at a diner as four Nazi skinheads walked by. They spotted us through the window and started blowing kisses and inviting us outside. It just seemed so clear that they loved one another's company and pretending to be gay in ironic and homophobic ways. Maybe it's oversimplifying the cause of their violence, but at that moment I couldn't help but think that if they could just fuck one another openly and proudly, it would make life better for all of us. A squad car rolled by and the Nazis hoofed it.

After a series of parole violations and weapons charges, and rumors of bomb-making material as well, they went back behind bars once again.

Here in Sacramento, we're pretty determined not to see them roaming about our downtown, posting up on corners and otherwise making our town feel safe for Nazis and no one else.

THE CLOWN WITH THE NAZI TATTOO

He was standing on the beach, sweating through his clown makeup, his "clown suit" just a baggy pair of Dickies work slacks, red Converse sneakers, and a Hawaiian shirt. He had no wig, just some messy hair around a sunburnt bald spot. It was love at first sight.

I was in Newport Beach as a promoter and emcee of the notorious Spike and Mike's Festival of Animation, and we were running our raunchy "Sick and Twisted" version of the show. As soon as I saw the hungover clown trying to sell balloon animals, hitting on girls, and striking out at both, I knew we needed him for the show.

"Hey man, how you doin'?" I approached him.

"I'm hot as fuck. How the hell are you doin'? Want a balloon monkey?"

"Ha. Yeah, me too, and no, thanks. Hey, you know how to make any dirty balloon animals?"

His bloodshot eyes lit up. I got the feeling this was the question he lived to hear.

"Oh yeah," he said, already readying a balloon—stretch, stretch, inflate with stale morning-after breath, and twist, twist, turn, bend, twist. "Voilà."

I was disappointed. I mean, it was a great bear, but just a bear. "That's not dirty. That's just a bear."

The showman was working his audience perfectly. He mimed confusion and sadness as he reached over to the bear's tail and gave a squeeze. The bear, to my delight and amazement, popped a boner as its clown father stared at me with a taunting "Say what now?" expression.

A balloon bear getting an erection on command was SO much more than I'd hoped for. I handed him the two bucks in my pocket and took the bear. "Bravo, sir!"

"I normally get three bucks for the dirty ones."

"Sorry, that's all I got. You want it back?"

"No. If you see me again later, give me a dollar."

"Hey, you ever heard of Spike and Mike's Festival of Animation?"

He had and was a fan. I arranged for him to meet me at the theater that evening with his balloons. He started listing off the other dirty balloon animals he could make: "Puppy with a boner, rabbit with a boner, cat with a boner, snake with a boner." The list was mostly animals with boners, and a dick-and-balls hat. A bikini-clad woman walked by and my new clown friend said a hasty good-bye to me. "Excuse me, ma'am, ya wanna see a cute little bear?"

I was pleasantly surprised when he actually showed up that night. I took to the stage.

"Do Spike and Mike love you?" I shouted. The crowd cheered.

"Do we love you enough to bring you the grossest, most depraved, offensive, vile animated shorts?"

The crowd went crazy.

"Do we love you so much that we would go down to the beach and find the most broken-down, hungover, sad wretch of a failed party clown to come here and make you pornographic balloon animals?" As the man who I still did not know by name walked onto the stage, the audience lost their damn minds.

He had a balloon dick hat on his head, balls hanging in his face, as he presented me with a boner bear to delight the fans. I let everyone know he was there for intermission working for tips or beers, and I implored them to be generous. The cartoons played to a happy and excited audience.

The clown was a big hit during intermission. With a handful of ones, he'd tell people he couldn't make change for their fives and twenties, and many people just went ahead and tipped him with the bigger bills.

Intermission ended and I was relaxing in the lobby having a beer and catching my breath. My clown friend approached, obviously heavily intoxicated.

"Keith, I gotta talk to you."

I was worried he didn't like the insulting introduction I'd intentionally not cleared with him ahead of time.

"Keith, brother, man, I have got to go on tour with you guys."

I knew that wasn't gonna happen. "Well, check with Spike. He does the hiring. I'll let him know you make the best boner bear around."

"Keith, Keith, this was the best, man. This was so great."

"Yeah, it looks like you made some cash."

"Tonight . . . changed my life. It changed my life." A little drunken hyperbole, I figured.

"I'm glad you had a good time."

"No, I mean it." He wiped a tear from his cheek. "This changed

51

my life. I made enough money to finally get my tattoo covered up and put my old life behind me."

"Oh?" This was intriguing. "What's your tattoo of?"

He looked around to be sure we were alone, which let me know it was gonna be good. He pulled up his shirt sleeve to reveal his soon-to-be-covered tattoo, a sloppily done red swastika. My eyes widened but I didn't have any words.

"That's not me anymore!" he insisted defensively. "That's my old life. I'm not like that. I love people, all people."

"Okay, okay, I believe you. What are you gonna cover it with?"

He reached into his back pocket, and I was delighted when he pulled out a tattered picture of Bozo the Clown and explained, "The red nose will cover the swastika perfectly." He gave me a big, drunken, clown hug and we went into the theater together to watch gross cartoons.

I still owe him a dollar.

"Assault is a crime. However, activists have been going to jail in support of worthy causes for hundreds of years. I have been to jail for marijuana activism (okay, possession) more than once. If someone feels it necessary to punch a confirmed Nazi, I support them in their act of self-defense."

—Ngaio Bealum, Activist, Comedian, Writer, and (Alleged) Puncher of Nazis

A FIGHT, A FIGHT, A MEXICAN, AND A WHITE

The way I heard it was, a group of white kids got into it with a group of Mexican kids at my junior high and things escalated until the whole school was abuzz with news that there was gonna be a huge Mexicans versus whites fight after school.

I wanted nothing to do with this. I hung out with a bunch of white kids who lived near the school, but I came from the same neighborhood as most of the Mexican kids and had been friends with many of them since kindergarten. I already felt like I'd betrayed my neighborhood when I stopped dressing like a break-dancer and started looking more like a member of Depeche Mode. I had no interest in further choosing sides.

The final bell rang and the school was electric, kids running every which way, some worrying and wanting to get the hell away from whatever was gonna happen, others trying to calm things down, and too many punching their fists into their hands and getting pumped up in a most macho way.

I saw my brother Edward and his friend Steve Vargas, two of

the toughest kids at Auburndale Junior High, strutting through the chaos and I ran over to them.

"Where are you guys going?" I panted at them.

Edward answered cheerfully, "To the fight."

"To the fight?!" Edward was white. Steve was Mexican. "What side are you two fighting on?"

Steve smiled at me and with a laugh in his voice said, "We're gonna hit EVERYONE."

In a panic, I implored Edward to get on the bus with me and go home.

He dismissed my concerns. "I'll be okay. Go catch your bus. I'll see you at home later."

I knew I wouldn't change his mind so I hurried to the front of the school where the buses were waiting for us. There I saw the street lined with beautiful old lowrider cars, mostly Chevys, and in each was at least two full-grown Mexican men, dudes with tattoos, the top buttons buttoned on their dress shirts, dark shades, lookin' like they meant business. At the sight of this, every would-be white brawler got on their bus or turned and walked back into the school to leave later when the way was clear.

It seems the white kids thought this was a game while the Mexican kids, and their fathers and uncles, saw something more serious, and they weren't having it. This is a pattern I'd see repeatedly when it came to racial conflict; online trolls just in it for the lulz, or the kid in a Charlottesville white-power rally tearing off his racist uniform and announcing, "I'm not a white supremacist! I was just in it for the laughs!" and, even more serious, white nationalists not understanding, or claiming not to understand, the anger they inspire in people who deal with the very real effects of racism daily.

Edward and Steve went and hung out with the unopposed Mexicans, and I hear it was quite a party.

FORGIVE ME FATHER FOR I HAVE SINNED

"How long since your last confession?"

"Uh . . . like thirty years at least."

"What do you wish to confess?"

"When I was eighteen years old I passed up a chance to see Econochrist, Filth, Sam I Am, and Green Day, so that I could go see Social Distortion instead."

"Leave."

"Excuse me?"

"Leave this holy place now, ya bastard! Go from here, and never return. May your soul burn in eternal hellfire!"

GREEN DAY WON'T PLAY SACTO

"In the Green Day *Slappy* 7-inch EP liner notes, it says, 'GREEN DAY WON'T PLAY SACTO,'" Corbett Redford informs me. He sits in his home office in Pinole, California, part of the East Bay Area adjacent to San Francisco, surrounded by records, graphic novels, collectible toys, books, and punk rock posters and flyers.

Just weeks earlier his documentary *Turn It Around: The Story of East Bay Punk* had its world premiere. The film features a key scene where legendary Berkeley, California, punk venue 924 Gilman receives an unwanted visit from a gang of Nazi skinheads. The true story comes to a thrilling conclusion when the Gilman regulars band together and attack the Nazis, with fists, baseball bats, skateboards, maybe a chair or two, and drive them off for good.

Corbett welcomed me into his home to share another story with me—one that, due to time constraints, ended up having to be cut from his final film. But first we chat about our respective scenes and the racist boneheads that plagued them. While

Sacramento had a bad reputation, the East Bay's punk shows had their share of problems with white supremacists.

I receive a thorough and enthusiastic lesson in the history of racist assholes of the greater East San Francisco Bay Area. I learn about white-pride gangs like the West Santa Rita Boys and their "War Wagon," a badass girl gang called the Durant Mob Rules that sprang up to fight back against skinheads, and Corbett sums it all up beautifully: "I know that members of Isocracy, Green Day, Possessed, Primus, Metallica, Corrupted Morals, all these people over the course of two and a half, three decades, systematically got their asses kicked in El Sobrante."

I'm eager to get to the cut footage, but I had to ask Corbett about a scar on his arm that he described to me as his "skinhead wound."

He rubs his forearm and recollects how it came to be so marked. "Well, it was 1998. There was a party in El Sobrante and it was at the old Digital Underground house."

Corbett had gone with a group of women including his girlfriend to see The Fleshies, an Alternative Tentacles–signed band that was a sister band to his own group, Bobby Joe Ebola and the Children MacNuggits.

A skinhead showed up as The Fleshies were doing their thing. Their thing involved John, their lead singer at the time, being completely naked as he performed. The skinhead took a commanding position at the front of the crowd, a tattoo across his shirtless back letting everyone standing behind him know that he takes pride in being white. While his first response was to be amused by the naked man on the microphone, it quickly got to be too much for him. "He picks up a basketball that happens to be in the house, and he just starts pegging the naked singer like he just can't stand the weirdness. He just can't deal with it."

From there this charming man with the shaved head started smacking other audience members with the ball, mostly women. Including smacking Corbett's friend V in the back of the head, and telling her she looks like a man.

A group of guys led the thug out into the backyard, to give him a firm talking to, but Corbett thought he deserved a bit more than a verbal scolding. "I got a couple stouts in me, and I'm a little short guy, maybe I have this Napoleon thing or something, I was so mad, I was just so, so mad that he had hit my best friend of thirty-five years and you know he'd hit two girls and there's nobody really doing anything."

Corbett headed for the backyard and confronted the skinhead, telling him he needed to "fucking knock it off." Corbett was asked just what he thought he could do about it, and, despite being at a huge size disadvantage, he took a swing at the skinhead. "I pushed 'Select' like little Joe on Mike Tyson's *Punch-Out* and I hit him with everything I had."

What Corbett didn't know was that his bandmate Dan had seen this coming and gotten down on all fours behind the bald giant, while another friend, Nema, stood by gripping a corkscrew.

The proud white man fell backward over Dan, landing in a recycling bin, and that's when things stopped going Corbett's way.

"He came up with a bottle, cracked it over my head, slashed my arm, and he went to stab my stomach. Dan stood up and blocked the bottle from gutting his friend, but things were still getting worse. Nema pulled out his corkscrew, and the skinhead snatched it from him and stabbed him in the neck. Then he upped the makeshift weapon ante, pulling out a BBQ shear. I was like, "What did I do? Why did I do this?"

Corbett was pushed quickly out of the house, being told that he'd fucked with the wrong guy, a bully who locals had long lived in fear of. "You don't even understand! That's the guy in our town who, ya know, like he's a white supremacist who took all of our lunch money and he always carries a gun. You don't understand what you've done!"

Meanwhile, a bunch of kids had surrounded the skinhead in the backyard and were beating the shit out of him with their skateboards, definitely one of my favorite weapons.

After driving himself to the hospital, Corbett sat bleeding for several hours in a crowded waiting room before giving up on the American approach to medicine and heading home to apply some butterfly bandages himself.

"The trigger in the waiting room was that everyone was watching *Mad TV* and there was some gag of some dude getting kicked in the balls and everybody was completely silent in that waiting room until that happened and everyone started laughing. I don't know what that was but when everyone started laughing at some dude getting kicked in the balls on TV I'm like, I'm out of here."

With this harrowing tale told, and my adrenaline flowing, I was ready to see the footage I'd come for. Corbett pulled up clips for me, and a series of interviews told the story of an infamous night when the East Bay Punks met the Sacramento Nazi Skins.

A promoter in Sacramento had booked the top acts from the East Bay punk scene, including legendary bands Econochrist, Green Day, Crummy Musicians, Filth, and Sam I Am.

And most of the East Bay bands that weren't playing had at least a member or two who made the trip up to enjoy the show and support their friends.

Ben Sizemore of Econochrist described feeling some trepidation ahead of the show. "Sacramento had a reputation, for having, well, it was kind of thought of as a redneck town, and it had Nazi skinheads."

Sizemore and the other Bay Area punks had heard about an incident that took place on August 21, 1990, when racist skinhead Michael G. "Iron Mike" Ortiz stabbed Paul Carrallo and Aragorn Moser outside the Cattle Club. Carrallo, twenty years old, died in the hospital the following day.

Econochrist and their friends made the trip despite these concerns. "Back then, you know, you feel invincible. You don't think anyone can hurt you. We were the East Bay Punks! We'll go up to Sacramento." Sizemore had a reputation of his own as a firebrand antiracist skinhead who didn't back down from a fight.

Piling a dozen or more people in a battered Ford Econoline van with expired tags, no insurance, and questionable breaks, they drove the ninety minutes or so to Sacramento.

The members of Green Day recall it being a really fun show, where they had transported the heart of their scene into a neighboring town. The bands shared equipment and, rather than do a standard format show, they just took turns playing a few songs each and then swapping out.

The fun came to an end when a group of skinheads showed up and started pushing their way through the crowd.

Green Day were on stage when pushing turned to punching and a fight broke out. A confusing scene, where multiple group fights were taking place throughout the room, got more confusing, as Green Day's bass player Mike Dirnt disappeared from the stage, jumping into the melee.

Sizemore remembers coming up against a seemingly invulnerable brute. "I remember getting a running start and throwing a chair at this guy, one of these Nazis. He was Sieg Heiling at the time and it just hits him in the face and knocks him down. He was such a badass he just stood up, broke the chair, and threw it back at me. 'Oh Shit!'"

In the middle of the chaotic violence, Billy Joe Armstrong and drummer John Kiffmeyer stood on stage, trying to figure out how to respond, when a group of young girls, seemingly oblivious to the rumble, approached the stage and asked the band if they'd be selling merch.

The crowd managed to push the Nazis out of the main hall but in the lobby things stalled. There, in a smaller, more controlled, space, their odds seemed a bit better and they planted their Doc Martens boots, refusing to take the remaining steps through the exit.

Green Day pal and unofficial roadie James Washburn lost his patience at this point. He described pushing his way to the front of the crowd, where he locked eyes with one skinhead, as another charged him from the side. Maintaining eye contact with the guy in front of him, he swung sideways and knocked the other guy out cold. Then, swinging a second time, he put a second skinhead on the ground.

Washburn's exploits that night are East Bay legend. Some of the musicians recall wanting to help but feeling like they were mostly just getting in his way.

James didn't come out of the melee completely unscathed. He broke a bone in his hand from punching someone.

Ben Sizemore recalls the excitement at sending the thugs running, and the ominous still that followed as he realized they weren't out of danger yet. "It was just awesome. It was like, Fuck these assholes, we kicked their ass. We are the punks! Fuck the Nazis . . . Shit, this is their town and they're probably gonna be back."

The members of Econochrist and their friends loaded up as fast as they could and got on the road. They still feel bad for not checking to make sure that everyone got on the road and out of harm's way.

Green Day were the last to leave. As they rushed to get their equipment into their vehicles, a couple of local cops arrived and yelled at them for being parked on the lawn. They told the two officers why they were there, and that there'd been a fight, and that a bunch of skinheads were on their way back. The cops listened to their story, told them to move their cars, and left. One punk who was there said, "That was the day I learned the difference between a Nazi skinhead and a cop. It's a mustache."

After their friends and the local police had left, they heard a terrifying sound, like an army coming down the street at full speed, running. Green Day and the other stragglers heard the thunder of Doc Martens hitting the ground, turned around, and saw a mob coming at them. There was no question who it was, or what they wanted. The punks scattered in every direction.

Billy Joe Armstrong narrowly escaped, a knife-wielding skinhead ripping his shirt off of him, as he ran.

The other band members had knives swung at them but managed to stay ahead of the bald attackers, taking off into the park.

Once the coast was clear, the scattered punks made their way back to find an ugly mess. One girl had her leg broken, the cars had smashed-in windows and slashed tires. They were ready to be back in the East Bay.

I missed the whole thing because I'd chosen to go see Social Distortion at the Cattle Club that night. Nazi skins fucked that show up too, as Mike Ness spent a lot of his time onstage mocking them as they Sieg Heiled him.

"That's adorable," he said to one of them. "You know, I used to fuck little boys like you in prison." I thought that claiming to fuck little boys was an odd way to insult someone, but Ness kind of pulled it off. Before Social Distortion had finished their set, the skinheads all took off. I didn't find out why until years later.

Many if not most of the East Bay Punks chose not to play Sacramento for quite some time. Green Day didn't return for several years, even printing "Green Day Won't Play Sacto" on the sleeve of one of their singles. They did eventually play the Cattle Club at the beginning of the Dookie Tour, just as they were blowing up into internationally famous rock stars. The show was without incident.

ANTIFA HQ AND GELATERIA

I went to Antifa's local headquarters to sign up.

They were in the most run-down mall in the south area, next to a frozen yogurt place. Frozen yogurt is gross. I want to wipe out racism, and sexism, and all the bad isms and phobias first, but then we should definitely do something about FroYo.

It would be cool if Antifa had gelato. I'll suggest it after I've been signed up longer. Gelato kicks FroYo's ass like Antifa kicks Nazi ass. That could be their slogan. Maybe I'll bring it up at the next rally.

I looked into signing up online, but I don't trust my credit card information on the Internet and they didn't take Bitcoin. So I headed down to their nearest storefront and perused the different plans available with cash in hand. I couldn't afford the full package, though it's cool that it comes with all-you-can-throw bricks.

I went ahead and got the junior membership. I'll still get the quarterly newsletter but I have to stand in the back during riots.

I grabbed a few Antifa t-shirts while I was there. Target has them cheaper but I wanted to support the cause. I said, "Thanks, comrade," to the dude ringing me up, and he gave me a dirty look. Was it really a dirty look, or is it like a secret handshake–type deal? So much to learn. I was bummed to find they don't offer lessons.

FOR REAL, THOUGH, SUPPORT YOUR LOCAL ANTIFA

If you think Antifa groups are as bad as Nazis, please stop being the right's tool.

Are you willing to take action against fascism? Great. You're Antifa. It's a broader term. It's loosely organized by design, which seems really hard for people to grasp, and so can also describe nonviolent action against fascism.

Stop saying they're as bad as Nazis. NO! Even if you disagree with them, being violent to people because they're gay, brown, Muslim, anything other than an able-bodied, white, cisgendered Christian man isn't "as bad" as being violent in response to this violence. Also, the Nazis are racking up quite a body count; Antifa are not, though they are being credited with defending many people from Nazi violence, in Boston and elsewhere.

Stop believing everything you read about them. Please remember violence will ALWAYS be overreported, false equivalencies will ALWAYS be drawn. Good deeds, like defending people, filming cops, putting their own bodies in the way of violence to protect people who came to protest peacefully in Boston (and elsewhere), will always be underreported. If it bleeds it leads.

They're not perfect. I have no doubt protestors/activists get carried away, make poor decisions, are dicks. But overall, they've been fighting Nazis way before most of us were even willing to recognize how bad our white nationalist terrorist problem is in this country. Hell, a lot of you still aren't there.

Antifa didn't just pop up overnight when Trump's presidential run started.

These white nationalists didn't just pop up overnight when Trump's presidential run started.

This fight has been going on for a long time. If you're new to it, welcome, maybe observe a bit more before forming strong opinions on how it should be fought.

I find a correlation among my friends and acquaintances: the more someone objects to confronting Nazis head-on, the greater the likelihood that they've never actually confronted or been confronted by a white supremacist.

I have had intelligent conversations with people who think the strategy of direct confrontation backfires, and works to demonize the left. I disagree, but I can see the reasoning. I enjoy these conservations. If someone opens with "Antifa are as bad as the Nazis," I know I'm not heading for a well-reasoned argument. And if someone says, "Antifa are the vegan ISIS" during a time when Antifa forces are literally fighting ISIS, I'm not gonna tune into their comedy news show as religiously as I used to.

To summarize, disagree with Antifa if you disagree with 'em, but do better at it.

The Daily show?

"Nazi Punks! Nazi Punks! Nazi
Punks! Let's talk!
Nazi Punks! Nazi Punks! Nazi
Punks! I support your freedom of
speech."

   —Not the Dead Kennedys

THE MASTER BASTARD

The center of the Sacramento punk scene when I was a kid was the Cattle Club, which operated inside of Bojangles, the city's first gay dance club. The venue seemed tailor-made for the rowdy shows I attended there religiously. The bar was separated from the rest of the venue, so they could sell alcohol but still have all-ages shows, and the club was just outside of downtown, close enough that you could manage to get there, but with no immediate neighbors to complain about the noise or the weird kids loitering about.

I started attending shows at the Cattle Club when I was sixteen. If the show was eighteen and over or sold out, or if I just didn't have any money, I'd sneak in by jumping the back wall, or by simply waiting until the front counter staff were too busy to notice me ducking past. The promoter, Fartie McFuckButt, would see me, knowing he hadn't seen me come in the front door. Sometimes he'd throw me out but usually he'd just sigh and shake his head.

Eventually he decided he'd had enough. "Keith, what do I got to do to get you to stop jumping the back wall?"

"Actually, a lot of the time I just sneak in when you're distracted."

"Keith . . ."

"Well, can't you just let me in? I'll pay when I can."

"Alright," he said, sounding defeated enough that I almost felt guilty for just a second.

"You pass out these flyers for me, and I'll let you in next show."

He'd have me pass out flyers now and then or do other small favors, but really, he asked very little of me. I have a feeling he saw a kindred spirit who just loved the music too much to stay away, even when broke.

Unfortunately, skinheads found the venue to their liking as well and were a constant presence.

While many shows were ruined by skinheads, I'd seen a few shows where the skinheads had been put in their place. One of my favorites was when the all-female punk band L7 played, and their majority female fan base just wasn't having it. Seeing tough, badass women in flannel shirts and ripped jeans pick a skinhead up and toss him across the room was a delight.

One night in particular stands out in my memory and continues to inspire me to this day.

Dennis Yudt served as the house deejay at the Cattle Club working under the name the Master Bastard. I loved the Bastard for his extensive record collection and his warped sense of humor, but most of all I loved the way he loved to piss off Nazis.

When the Doc-Martens-booted, close-shaved thugs would show up to fuck up shows and try to terrorize us, the Master Bastard, from his raised booth behind the stage, would play "Teddy Bear Picnic" over and over again, which made me laugh and for some reason drove the boneheads nuts. On this particular night he was getting them nice and riled up, and they were flipping him off and doing their cute little Sieg Heil routine in his direction. One of them got on stage as Dennis was giving "Take the Skinheads Bowling" by Camper Van Beethoven a spin and started making threats. Dennis looked at the loudmouthed, angry young man promising to do harm to his body and calmly took a drag off his cigarette. Then he flicked the cigarette, bouncing it off his would-be assailant's bald head. The little skinhead crew went nuts. They yelled, Sieg Heiled some more, made more threats, and overall did their chest-pounding best. Dennis started "Take the Skinheads Bowling" over and lit another cigarette. One of the skinhead girls, with a fringe haircut that I always thought was so cute I was bummed they gave it such a nasty association, flicked her own cigarette at Dennis. He stopped the music, pulled his mic to his mouth, and, sounding like a professional wrestler, yelled back, "You wanna flick cigarettes? I got a whole carton, assholes!" He then started lighting and flicking and lighting and flicking, multiple cigarettes at a time. The skinheads were getting angrier and angrier. Dennis was having fun, ducking, dodging, lighting, and flicking smokes. At some point he'd put "Teddy Bear Picnic" back on and turned it up. He was clowning and they were his marks, completely and sincerely enraged.

As funny as it was, I wondered where it would all go. Was I going to see Dennis get his ass kicked? Were the bands going to be able to play? Was I going to get my ass kicked?

Right when it looked like the scary bald men were going to take their anger out on those of us who were laughing in the audience, Dennis stopped the music abruptly, grabbed his mic, and yelled, "Listen here, boneheads, there are more of us than there are of you." They all yelled back at the same time, their words lost in a cacophony of anger and hate. Dennis clicked his mic back on. "There Are More of Us than There Are of You!" he yelled again.

"There Are More of Us than There Are of You!" He repeated it over and over again, and as we looked around, it dawned on us that he was right. They were bigger than most of us, and scarier, but not enough to make up for just how severely outnumbered they were. Then someone from the crowd started chanting along with Dennis. It was a Rudy runs the ball, or slow clap, or Rocky moment as more and more us started chanting along: "THERE ARE MORE OF US THAN THERE ARE OF YOU!"

We started to close in on them, chanting in their faces. They'd push one person who got too close and the rest of the crowd would surge forward toward them. And then, to my astonishment, they left. I don't even remember what bands played that night, but the crowd was pumped and we had a great time.

I called Dennis up recently at his current home in the Pacific Northwest to chat about the glory days of antagonizing racist skinheads. He was more than eager to tell these tales, but first he told me how he came to fall in with the punk scene in the late seventies and early eighties.

"It was just open door." Dennis spoke with the same measured, thoughtful, and even gentle voice that I remembered contrasting so delightfully with his aggression in the deejay booth. "You had, it was almost 50/50, men, women, lots of queers, blacks, it was open to weirdos, and people that were kind of on the fringes, people who liked to get into trouble, youthful offenders."

We both laughed, recognizing ourselves in that last category. Most notable in his recollection was the absence of any overt racism in the early days.

When rumors of Nazi punk and skinhead gangs in Huntington Beach and other Southern California cities reached Sacramento, the scene here quickly factionalized. "It became Punk

Rock with a capital P and a capital R and a little trademark and everyone had to have their uniforms on." Dennis was baffled to see such an open scene so easily fall to such impulses, that anyone could hear the same stories he heard of skinheads taking over shows, of fistfights and racist violence, and think, "Yeah, that sounds cool."

Despite being part Korean and Bohemian, he was, surprisingly, not targeted for harassment or abuse by the racist punks.

"I think part of it is being mixed race. I think I just confused people. I got away with telling people [I was] Icelandic."

Before moving to California, Dennis moved around a lot from one Air Force base to another, and he experienced plenty of racism at that time. "I always got beat up in elementary school all the way up through sixth grade. Those were hell years. Growing up on Air Force bases and you have, you know, a big, for lack of a better word, Southern contingency, going to those schools. Going to school when the TV show *Kung Fu* was on, so kids would come up to me and just start karate-chopping me, thinking that I'm gonna fight back and that I know kung fu because all Asians apparently are supposed to." Making things even worse was the Vietnam War still raging on, and racists not caring to distinguish between Korean and Vietnamese.

When punk came along, its radical inclusiveness was a godsend for Dennis. "Everything good in my life has come out of punk rock. It sounds cliché and silly and a tad nostalgic, which I certainly try not to be, but it really did save my life."

One of the people Dennis met in the Sacramento punk community was the Frank Sinatra- and Elvis-loving Fartie McFuck-Butt. The two quickly became best friends, and when Fartie decided to start a club, his friend with the eclectic record collection was a natural choice to deejay. After the first few months of more traditional record spinning, Fartie came to Dennis with a mission. "Fartie approached me and was like, 'You know what would be really funny is if we just turned on your microphone and you could start insulting the crowd.' It was Fartie's idea, the whole thing, the Master Bastard, he came up with the name, he came up with the persona and everything, and he just let me run with it, and that I did."

And that he did. I remember Dennis's misbehavior more than I remember the countless bands I went to see at the Cattle Club.

Fartie knew Dennis well enough to know he'd make a Master Bastard.

Dennis perked up when I reminded him of the rage he'd inspire by playing "Take The Skinheads Bowling" by Camper Van Beethoven for the Nazi skinheads whenever they'd show up.

"Nothing got under their skin like that. It was much more effective than playing, say, the Dead Kennedys' 'Nazi Punks Fuck Off' because it was funny, and if there's anything skinheads hate it's being laughed at."

To my surprise, in Dennis's view he was helping keep the peace. Fartie asked him to try and diffuse the situation when things got heated. "And my way of doing that is playing 'Take the Skinheads Bowling' and telling the crowd, 'Look around. There's five hundred of us, there's ten of them. We've got the upper hand. Laugh! Laugh at them. This is funny. This is funny. They think that they control us. We control them. We control the situation here.'"

I never thought of Dennis as diffusing anything, but I see that he's right, he did, and with integrity. Still, there were nights when he seemed less pure in his motives.

Dennis had a good hearty laugh when reminded of the cigarette wars. A heavy smoker, he'd often finish two packs of Lucky

Strikes in a single shift at the club. He insisted someone flicked a cigarette at him first, unwittingly inviting Dennis to show off a unique skill of his.

"I got really, really good at flicking cigarettes. That's how I would dispose of my butts. I could hit things from about fifteen to twenty feet away just through trial and error over many years. I got really, really good at flicking cigarettes unbeknownst to the person who was trying to hit me with theirs." Dennis had the skills, and he had plenty of ammunition, as well. "Every time I'd spot that guy, there it was, just 'POOF.' It was like my little Fourth of July celebration watching the plume of orange embers bouncing off of his back."

While Fartie received several severe ass-whoopings at the Cattle Club, the Master Bastard somehow came through unscathed. I wonder how he pulled this off.

He had a few close calls. On one occasion, when he'd been cornered by a group of Nazis, a man appeared just in time to rescue him. "He was wearing a yellow trash bag that they would use for CalTrans for like picking up trash, and he was like, 'You don't touch that guy.'" The guy was an old punk who'd turned skinhead but still remembered Dennis affectionately from the old days.

At the club, the mostly black security guards kept an eye out for Dennis. They bonded over their dislike of racist skins.

It's funny to realize the racist skins hung out at a place that was a part-time gay bar with a mostly black security staff and a half-Korean deejay.

I told Dennis how much it meant to me the night he led us all in chanting the Nazis out the door. "It was just a matter of logistics. It was a true thing. To have ten skinheads in a room full of three hundred nonskinheads. If you look at it logistically, that's not a fair fight, you know, ten against three hundred, yet people were intimidated. People wouldn't come together. And that was the thing. The skinheads were together as one force. It was the need to galvanize the rest of the people around them to realize, 'Oh, Fuck, yeah, why are we are we letting ten people control a crowd of three hundred?' I felt this necessity to point out 'There are more of us than there are of you. And we're not gonna let you ruin this show. We have control of the situation. If we wanted to we could turn on you at any given moment and beat the fuck out of you.'"

One thing that came across as Dennis recollected these conflicts was how much he cared about us, the kids just a few years younger than him coming into the punk scene. That skinheads would ruin that experience for us and get in the way of enjoying the music and camaraderie was something he would not tolerate.

I finished my call with Dennis, and a few short weeks later, on Friday, August 11, 2017, and Saturday, August 12, 2017, the alt-right gathered in Charlottesville, Virginia. They showed their hand, failing to maintain their "It's about heritage" and "Free speech" facade; they went full Nazi, chanting one of Hitler's favorites, "Blood and Soil," while marching with swastika flags and Sieg Heiling. Many showed up to oppose them, some peacefully, some with force, some identified as Antifa, some did not.

A white nationalist plowed his car into a crowd of pedestrians. Heather Heyer, thirty-two, of Charlottesville was killed, and nineteen others were injured.

The next week in Boston, a similar rally was overwhelmed by protesters. The Nazi demonstrators foolish enough to show up were vastly outnumbered. As former InfoWars reporter and all-around Nazi asshole Joe Briggs tweeted from Boston, "We are huddled around in the common waiting to find out if we have police protection or if we have to fight our way out. This is America," I thought of Dennis. I thought, "Yeah, this is America, and there's more of us than there are of you."

"When white people tell you that you need to debate Nazis to persuade them, what they're really saying is that the Nazi viewpoint is worthy of debate. And you have to wonder why they would believe that."
    —Cate Gary, Comedian/Trumpslayer

RAINBOW NAZI

My girlfriend, Rachel, and I were living in a VW bus as we toured the United States. It was 1994, and driving through the South still made me nervous.

I tour across the United States frequently now and have come to realize that the South isn't actually in the south. It's about fifteen miles outside of any major metropolitan area.

Our first stop in Texas was for gas. I had bleached hair, starting to dread in places (Yeah, I know. I promise you, I am sufficiently embarrassed), and Rachel's hair was cut very short and died an eggplant shade of purple. I had a Public Enemy cassette tape blaring on the sound system.

Looking at the trucker-capped driver of the big four-wheel-drive that pulled in next to us, I thought it might be wise to turn down the loud voice of Chuck D before opening my door. I decided to just let it play and hopped out to fill up with gas.

Trucker Cap had his window open as he filled his tank, music blaring from his truck. We looked at each other and laughed, realizing we were playing the same album. He wished me a good night in his Texan accent as he headed out.

I relaxed a bit, and we enjoyed the southern leg of our epic journey. Eventually we reached Tallahassee, Florida, where we stayed with Bill and Rob, a gay couple I'd met when their own cross-country VW journey had brought them out to our coast. After hanging out with two gay men, going camping, even doing a bit of nightclubbing, we were able to forget we weren't in our liberal West Coast town. We'd be reminded where we were soon enough.

We said good-bye to our friends and headed toward Atlanta. The café we stopped at for lunch was packed with a large group of people wearing matching shirts. We figured them for a family reunion and we smiled at the kids as we enjoyed our meal.

A giant of a man in a straw hat gave us a friendly hello, and we exchanged smiles as he made his way to the bathroom. He passed close enough for me to read what was written on his t-shirt, particularly the official-looking script across the bottom: "Fraternal Order of The White Knights of The Ku Klux Klan."

My stomach dropped. I wanted my smile back. I wanted him to know he disgusted me. I also wanted to make it out of Florida alive. We left money on the table to cover our food and a tip and got out of there.

An hour or so later I pulled over on the shoulder of the highway after spotting a hitchhiker. Not picking up hitchhikers just felt wrong when driving a VW Camper Bus. They always stood a little taller and looked so hopeful when they saw you coming. He ran to catch up with the bus, and as he reached the open passenger-side window where Rachel was seated, he looked in, said "thank you," and then, taking a better look, "Keith?"

Rachel laughed hard at this. She couldn't get through a grocery store without her social butterfly boyfriend running into a dozen people he knew, and now, having driven across a continent, we still hadn't escaped the phenomenon.

The hitchhiker turned out to be Rainbow Joe, who knew me from when I emceed Spike and Mike's Animation Festival in Tallahassee the year prior. We told him we were heading to Atlanta and he asked if we'd like to check out a Rainbow Gathering. I'd heard of these hippie campouts and our schedule was flexible. Rachel moved to the backseat as we let Joe take over navigation duties.

Getting to the state park was easy enough, with a quick stop to buy a fifty-pound bag of beans and another of rice, and several big jugs of water. Inside the park the directions were a bit harder to follow, with unmarked streets, or signs blocked by trees, and it had gotten dark.

Rachel went to sleep in the back, and Joe and I did our best to follow the directions that had been recorded on a tape and that he was now playing back through a small handheld recorder. There was some ambiguous wording and we started to worry. It seemed odd to me that there was no sign of a large gathering. Joe kept having to rewind the tape to make sure we didn't miss a detail, then suddenly I heard my own voice on the recorder saying, "Shit man, are we lost?" He'd accidentally hit record, putting my voice in place of what turn we were supposed to take next. We soldiered on.

It was a kind of dark that my city-boy eyes didn't know what do with. We'd go up a hill, and as we'd crest the space in front of us would be a black void. You'd assume there was going to be street in front of you when the headlights finally reached the ground, and there was, until there wasn't. We hit a ditch, hard, and fifty pounds of beans, fifty pounds of rice, and all the water came crashing down on my poor sleeping girlfriend, who pledged never to let anyone else be the navigator ever again.

We called it a night and folded out the camper bed, which we then shared with a stranger we'd just picked up hitchhiking. In the morning, we had a dead battery.

I hoofed it to the nearest houses and started knocking on doors hoping to get a jump start. Most folks wouldn't even open their doors, just hollering to me from the other side that they couldn't help me. I walked back toward the bus defeated, wondering how we were going to push-start since we were parked in a ditch. A beat-up pickup truck pulled over and asked me if I was the guy with the dead battery. They looked like the South. They looked like central casting's idea of the South if they were making a *Texas Chainsaw Massacre* remake. I hopped in their truck and they took me to my bus. They gave us a jump, and they knew just where we were heading. "You guys looking for the Rainbow Gathering?" They pointed us in the right direction and promised they'd be by later.

The Rainbow Gathering was wonderful. I parked between other VW buses and helped Joe carry in the beans, rice, and water. A cooking station and dishwashing station had been set up, and they were efficient and well organized. Volunteers cooked and cleaned, and everyone pitched in. I signed up to do some dishes, after we filled our stomachs. People in floral print dresses, tie-dyed t-shirts, and corduroys played frisbee and hacky sack, taught each other crafts, and drummed in a big circle. I made fun of them, of course I did, but I enjoyed the hell out of this scene. This was the part of hippie culture they got right. It was inclusive, and community-building, and maybe it wasn't going to change the world, but it was a pretty great way to take some rest and recharge. Rachel and I explored the woods for a bit and then caught a nap in some hammocks. Everyone came together for dinner. There was a group howl and a quick meeting to address any concerns. The locals who'd charged our battery showed up and were asked politely if they could come back without the guns mounted on their trucks. They agreed happily and headed home to drop off their rifles.

I grabbed a plate of rice and veggies, poured a thick bean stew over it, and grabbed a seat around the campfire next to a delightful old hippie who invited me to call her Grams.

Grams asked me if it was my first gathering. I told her it was and was rewarded with great stories of the gatherings she'd attended over the decades. I listened to her stories, and shoveled food in my mouth, sitting at a campfire in a beautiful forest in Georgia at dusk, and I felt very glad to have picked up that hitchhiker. This was a lovely place to be.

Looking around the circle, I spotted one young man trying to get the hang of a hand drum. He had a crudely tattooed swastika and the letters "SWP," which I knew to stand for Supreme White Power (sorry, Sherwin-Williams Paints). "Who brought the Nazi?" I muttered to Grams.

"I did," she answered.

I looked at her, surprised.

Grams explained to me that her grandson had made friends with the neighbor boy, whose parents were white supremacists. She had to make a decision. If she told him he couldn't be friends with this young man, she'd not only feel like a hypocrite, she might push him into that world as happens when something is forbidden to a teenager.

So, her grandson and this young man were friends, and he was regularly at their house, where he was exposed to different cultures via music, food, and frequent houseguests.

"And his parents let you bring him here?" I asked.

"They did. I promised them I'd see that our kids behaved and that I'd keep him safe."

"Wow." I had to think about the logic behind this approach for a minute. "Would you let your grandson go to a white-power rally with them?"

She thought about this for a moment. "I really don't know. Paul's pretty secure in loving all people. Maybe he'd do some good . . . yeah, I don't know if I would."

I looked at the little Nazi spawn, sitting next to his friend Paul and a black man who was giving him tips on playing the hand drum.

This was the best Nazi punch I could imagine, taking their kids.

OUTRAGE

had a cable public access show way before *Wayne's World*. *Local Trash* brought the citizens of Roseville, California, the very best of fifteen-year-olds smashing out three-chord punk rock while yelling in delightful adolescent voices about bored cops, asshole teachers, and posers.

I was a mess of depression and anger at moving from Southern California, where I'd known one house as home all my fourteen years, to Roseville, a suburb of Sacramento, where I knew no one and got made fun of for my weird clothes. My mom, saint that she is, saw an ad, "Public access producers needed. Free training!" and encouraged me to call. Once again, Mom saved my life.

I learned to operate a camera, work a switcher, and I was probably one of the last people to learn to edit video using two tape decks and a controller. I spent many happy hours entering edit in and out points at RSVL8, our local cable access station, set up by the cable company as part of their deal with the city to bring cable TV to our market.

And unlike other geeky hobbies I'd undertaken, this one actually made me friends, though perhaps not the friends my dear sweet mom would have chosen for me. Soon I knew most every teenage metal or punk musician in town.

I got a call inviting me to come meet a band called American Freedom. A friend was persuaded to drive me to a house in a nearby suburb where they were rehearsing. The first thing I noticed after walking into the backyard was skinheads. I'd never actually met a skinhead. I'd always thought they looked cool, in fact their uniform reminded me of the cholos I'd grown up with, but the kind of over-the-top masculinity they represented was something I'd never been a fan of. It turned out that two of the skinheads were the singer and the guitarist in the band. I just assumed they were "the good kind," and as I started up the camera this was one of the first things they confirmed. "We're SHARPS, Skinheads Against Racial Prejudice," the guitarist, Sam, announced. Ryan, a friend of the band, chimed in, "Yeah, man, fuck Nazis. Hitler's dead."

That was all I needed to hear. They started playing heavily Minor Threat–influenced punk rock and I loved it and recorded it. Once again, the big shoulder-killing camera I signed out from RSVL8 had made me some new friends.

They invited me to see them play at a backyard party that weekend. I stood on the edge of a mosh pit after running out of videotape, and a caveman-looking punk with a Mohawk stopped in front of me. "I'm Rot," he said, holding up his fist where he had tattooed the letters R O T between his knuckles.

"I'm Keith," I answered, feeling bad that I didn't have it written on me anywhere. Rot put his arm around me and pulled me into the pit. It was one of the nicest ways anybody has ever welcomed me into a new group.

It was decided that I would become the band's manager, and thankfully they also decided to change their awful name.

American Freedom became Outrage. I didn't have a very clear idea of what a manager was meant to do. I attended rehearsals, made t-shirts by hand using special crayons that could be ironed into permanence. I shot music videos for them, one of which had the distinction of generating the most complaint calls and letters RSVL8 Public Access had ever received. Chris, who ran the studio, thanked me for confirming that people were actually watching. The offending video featured footage of people doing drugs, made extra realistic because Jon the bass player was diabetic and we were able to make use of his syringes. Our defense was that the message of the song "Sick Man" was an antidrug one.

During this time, I was working at Kentucky Fried Chicken, shooting and editing my cable access show, and sleeping through most of my classes at school.

My history teacher, Mr. Shields, pulled me aside after class. "Keith, I don't know what's going on in your personal life, but you know this material, you've obviously done the reading. I'd rather you didn't sleep in my class, but I understand we all gotta sleep sometime. If you can get an A on every Friday test and on your final, and you do all your homework, you can sleep through class and still get a C."

"And without the homework?" I asked, being realistic.

"With all As on the weekly tests and on the final, you can get a D without homework."

I thanked him and went for the D.

I was with Jon and Sam, the bass player and the guitarist, in the tiny editing suite at RSVL8, which was literally a closet. Crammed together in tight quarters, I couldn't help but notice that Sam was squirming in his chair and pulling at his pants.

"Hey man, you okay?" I asked. "You got crabs?"

"No, I don't have fucking crabs," he snapped. "I shaved my balls and they itch."

Jon and I started to giggle. "You shaved your balls?" I squeaked.

"I'm a fucking skinhead!" Sam answered, as if it were obvious.

Jon and I picked up that he was pretty angry and we tried to go back to editing. Sam was a solid, muscular dude and I didn't think I could take him in a fight. I had no desire to find out. We did our best to stifle our giggles.

A few minutes later my curiosity got the better of me. "Skinheads shave their balls?" Jon lost his battle against the giggles and let out a loud, explosive laugh.

"YES!"

"So all skinheads do this?"

"YES! Real skinheads shave their balls."

At that we laughed openly. Picturing these big, tough dudes with smooth, clean balls was just too much. Sam punched us both hard in the arm. We tried to stop. We tried to get back to work. But the giggle kept creeping up whenever Sam would shift or scratch at himself. Finally he'd had enough. "Fuck you guys," he said, and he stormed out of the editing closet.

None of us mentioned this again. I helped Outrage record a demo. It was an exciting day. We listened to the tape in my parents' van immediately after and the band members' parents held a meeting to discuss how to support their kids, which was kind of amazing.

But . . . the band broke up, and, shortly after, Sam started a new band with his skinhead friend Ryan, the one who had reminded us on camera that Hitler was dead the day I'd first been introduced to this crowd. I was surprised and saddened to find out they were a white-power band. I went to see them perform at a garage party to see for myself if it was true. It was.

They had flipped their ideology 180 degrees. They went from antiracist to racist and didn't even have to change their uniforms other than swapping out their shoelaces for white ones.

I'd had Sam over to my house when my parents were entertaining black and Mexican friends, my dad having to whisper the explanation that there were apparently good skinheads, too. I knew this would be the end of our friendship. I certainly would never welcome him into my home again.

I got good and drunk at the show and climbed into the camper-shelled bed of a pickup truck with Jon, who had played bass for Outrage, and several other punks. We were quiet as the truck pulled away from our friend's white-power coming-out party. Our buddy had gone over to the dark side. I figured I'd never see Sam again, and this turned out to be true.

Then, lying drunk in the back of a pickup truck, I started to defend racism. This was a game I often played in my own head, picking a position I found abhorrent and then trying to argue it to sharpen my debate skills and my own position. I had to be pretty drunk to play this little game out loud.

Jon, who I remember as intelligent, kind, and gentle, said firmly, "Keith, shut up."

I did and we rode the rest of the way in silence.

"Punching someone should make you uncomfortable. It's an important moral decision that shouldn't be taken lightly. Punching a Nazi should make you uncomfortable too, because you should hit them hard enough that your hand hurts afterwards."

—Dan Arel, Author, Award-Winning Journalist

RYAN

I met Ryan on my first day at Oakmont High School.
I'd been kicked out of Roseville High, the other high school
in town, transferring to a "continuation school," which is the
modern equivalent of reform school, the school behind the
school, the school housed in trailers, like they're trying to get
us used to living that way, the school with the day care facility,
and also the school with the awful name, always, continuation
schools have the worst names, like they didn't want to waste a
good name on us. I went to Success High, which is either very
optimistic or just the product of someone's mean sense of irony.

"I know, let's call the school with all the burnouts and screw-
ups 'Success,' ha ha ha." It was a perfect name, though, two
words, Success High, the thing we would likely not achieve, and
the reason why.

I was one of a small percentage who made their way out of the
continuation school system back into regular school. All it took
was getting punched by a guy who thought I was flirting with his
wife. Yes, his wife, in high school. I was flirting with her a bit, but
more like I was her gay BFF. She like burly bad boys, which I was

not. I was a skinny guy who liked a lot of "faggy" music. I also arranged her a ride to a free clinic and went with her for comfort and support when he'd managed to knock her up, something he never knew about. If he had been privy to this information, perhaps he'd have been more tolerant of a little friendly flirting.

Instead, his fist connecting with my jaw hard enough to spin me around marked me as a punching bag, and a week later another student decided he'd have a go at me with very little provocation.

I was in art class, making a Pink Floyd, *The Wall*–themed mug. Glenn and his cousin Sandy were hurling insults at each other across the class. Sandy was sitting right next to me, and every time she called her cousin a "gap-toothed, chicken fucker, redneck piece of shit," it took me right out of the Pink Floyd vibe I was trying desperately to hang onto.

Glenn called her a "fat cunt," and I knew from the big breath she took in that her reply was going to be a loud, long one. I interrupted, "Hey, Sandy, I'm trying to work. Could you maybe go fight with your cousin over there, where he's sitting." She looked at me in disgust.

"What the fuck did you just say to my cousin?" Glenn yelled from his table.

"What? I just asked her if she could fight with you without me in between you guys."

"You think you can talk to my cousin like that?!" he raged.

"Talk to your cousin like what? You just called her a cunt."

And that was the switch. Glenn turned bright red. "YOU CALLIN' MY COUSIN A CUNT?"

"What?! No! I didn't. You did."

"That's it. I'm gonna fucking kill you after class. You are dead."

This was all yelled at top volume, in a class with the teacher

96

present. Mr. Fox didn't seem to notice. The bell rang and the class emptied. I moved against the tide of students to Mr. Fox's desk. "Hey, um, Glenn and his friends are waiting outside to beat me up," I informed him, hoping to wake him out of the coma he seemed to be in.

"Yeah? Sorry about that."

"Well, can you help me? Walk me to the office?"

"No. Sorry. They'd just go right around me."

"Well, can you call Mr. Litke?" Litke was our principal, and a good ally.

"Nope. Phone's busted."

"Well, can you do anything for me at all?"

"I'm afraid not. You can try going out the back door."

I made a note to spit in Mr. Fox's coffee next chance I got and tried the back door. The way was clear. I figured I would run toward the office, and by the time Glenn and his thugs saw me I'd have a good head start. I took a deep breath and bolted.

As I rounded the corner I heard, "There he is, get him!" I was already running as fast as my legs could go.

I reached the office door, ran inside, and then stood, waiting. Glenn came whipping around the corner, fully enraged, and as he lunged toward me, I swung the metal door hard, smashing him in the face.

I ran through the front office into the principal's office and again stood in the doorway.

"Keith, what's going on?" Litke asked.

Just then Glenn came into sight again, blood pouring from his nose and mouth. Again he lunged, and again I managed to smash him in the face with a door. I then reached down and locked the door, and as Litke came around his desk I grabbed his phone and called my mom.

"Come get me. Now."

Litke told me to stay put and went to try and calm Glenn, who was now pounding on his door yelling threats, and figure out what had happened. He knew both students well enough to assume that I was most likely acting in self-defense. I wasn't interested in talking to him for fear that I'd start sobbing.

I watched through a window for my mom's van and then beelined it from the office. Litke followed me, and my mom asked him what was going on.

"I don't know. Keith isn't ready to talk about it. Give me a call later."

I gave my mom the whole story and I informed her that I was done. I would not be going back to that school. My dad had other ideas and arranged a meeting with Litke. On the day of the meeting, Dad got his first look at my schoolmates and changed his tune immediately.

"Keith doesn't belong here. These kids look like convicts, adult convicts. Keith just has a big mouth."

The faculty agreed. I'd been a good student, and they decided it was time to give me another shot at attending a regular high school.

And so I was enrolled at Oakmont High School, the only school in our town I hadn't yet sampled. I was glad to be away from the prison-yard mentality of continuation school, but I wasn't thrilled to be starting over again with no friends. Then I spotted Ryan.

Sitting by himself in plaid pants and a flannel, his long Mohawk down over half his face.

I just sat next to him. Our clothes and the musical tastes they were associated with said that we were supposed to be friends. This schoolyard tribalism has always baffled my dad but it served a purpose.

Ryan was very skinny, and he had bulgy eyes. We often teased him that he looked like a mosquito. "I have clogged tear ducts! I was born premature," he'd explain, to anyone and everyone. This was his excuse anytime he was driving people crazy, like when he had trouble ordering at Taco Bell, the old lady taking our order giving him her sympathy and maybe an extra taco.

Ryan may be the sincerest person I've ever met. Logic and truth meant everything to Ryan. And as a result, his mouth would get him into conflicts he was not physically fit to deal with.

As I sat on the cement next to him and leaned back against the wall, he just started talking as if we were old friends. "Look at this lunch. Who would feed this to their kid? My mom is the worst." He had a sandwich consisting of two pieces of white bread and one piece of bologna. He took the one sad round disc of processed meat byproduct, and he flung it absentmindedly. We both heard the splat and looked up to see that the offending piece of meat product had struck a girl easily a foot taller than us in the face before landing on the cement between our boots and her sneakers.

"Why did you do that?" she asked.

"I thought you looked hungry," Ryan answered.

We exchanged names and became friends as we ran from her, having to jump a fence before she finally gave up on kicking our asses. It felt like he hadn't intended to be mean but just had no control over his mouth. This would be confirmed over time.

Ryan would confront skinheads, and anyone else who he disagreed with. He'd be very logical in his argument, more often than not resulting in them calling names, attacking his character, or threatening to kick his ass. This too he'd respond to logically, like a punk rock Mr. Spock. "Why are you insulting me? That isn't a good rebuttal. Do you have a rebuttal? You're incorrect, I'm not gay, but that doesn't have anything to do with what we're talking about. You're threatening me with violence now. Does that mean you can't answer my question?"

Even people who like to hit other people will puff up their chests and try to get some kind of return huff, some physical response that will help them justify throwing a punch. Ryan confounded them. He would not change his body posture, not defensively or aggressively, and would just keep his mouth going. He'd put them in a position to look really bad if they hit him, and it was beautiful. I didn't know how far it could go. When the other party started looking like they were gonna deck him regardless, one of us would start walking Ryan away, usually to the relief of whatever bully he was arguing with. And even as we escorted him away from the scene, the mouth would be going, going, going.

One night we were at a warehouse that had been a church that later became an all-ages dance club. As things were closing down a batch of Nazi skins showed up, as they always did.

Ryan decided to engage. He wanted to know why they came to dance clubs when they didn't dance. He wanted to know how they justified thinking white people are superior when they themselves didn't have very many exemplary traits to speak of. A whole group of them, maybe a half dozen, was standing around him as he took them on in debate using all of his usual tactics.

I was trying hard to convince him to leave, while strategically not standing where the half circle of skins could close in on me. One of them prided himself on being an intellectual and he tried to take Ryan on. He didn't stand a chance and the guy got angrier and angrier. One of them turned to me and said, "You better get him the fuck out of here, now."

I worried it was too late as the would-be intellectual bonehead stepped forward and gave Ryan a hard shove. Ryan used the backward momentum to run, but there was nowhere to run, they had him against the wall. He jumped and grabbed the carpet that had been hung on the wall as a sound barrier, and it came down on top of him. He grabbed one edge of it and started rolling back toward the skinheads. The carpet rolled up around him, wrapping him up like a burrito. The skinheads hopped over it, and one or two gave a sloppy kick in its direction. Ben and I reached down and grabbed the Ryan burrito, picked it up, and told the bald guys, "We'll take care of him," as we hurried out the door. We threw the package in the back of Ben's car and drove off, Ryan once again escaping unscathed other than a few rug burns.

GERALDO'S NOSE CATCHES A CHAIR

In 1988 I watched with my parents as embarrassed investigative journalist-*cum*-daytime talk show host Geraldo Rivera got his nose get smashed in by a chair during a live taping of the TV show that bore his name.

A group of obnoxious, pretty-boy Nazis sat on the *Geraldo* stage calling people "kikes" and "Uncle Tom" until finally another guest, a black activist named Roy Innis, rose from his seat and put his hands around white supremacist John Metzger's throat. All hell broke out at this point, and that's when Geraldo caught a chair with his face.

I immediately said that Innis was in the wrong, infuriating my father. I had skinhead friends at this point, which concerned my parents, but they believed me when I explained that they were SHARP skinheads, antiracists. I think at this moment my dad had his doubts.

"He lost the moral high ground by getting violent. Of course he was right before that, and they were wrong, but he let them provoke him. He got violent first."

My dad let his anger stop him from being as eloquent or persuasive as he might otherwise have been. "They called him an Uncle Tom! They were calling people kikes."

"So what!" was my thoughtful rebuttal. Which pissed my dad off more.

So what, indeed. My sixteen-year-old brain couldn't fathom the violent history of those words. I saw this as an isolated incident, removed from years of racial violence and oppression.

On a certain level I was right. Ideally Innis would have continued to take them down intellectually, strategically this might have been better for him, but to think that I could imagine being in his shoes with a smug, privileged twenty-year-old trying to yield that kind of power over me, to assume that I could sit there and maintain the calm, intellectual "high ground," was naive.

This kind of arrogance about racism on the part of white people is unfortunately common. The first time I heard of Prince, the VJ of our local music video show, *MV3*, said that Prince claimed MTV wasn't playing his videos because he was black, and ten-year-old me thought, *This guy sounds like a real whiner.* At ten years of age something gave me the confidence to believe that I had more authority on the subject of racial discrimination than a black artist. Then they played "Little Red Corvette," and I thought, *Yeah, MTV ought to be playing this. They ARE racist.*

Back to Geraldo, there was even more at play here on the part of Huey, Louie, and Adolph, sitting on that stage espousing their racism, than historic violence. The modern-day groups and movements they represented were famously violent and well documented as such.

Even their costumes were militaristic. Them boots were made for kicking. The great strategy of the Civil Rights Movement in the sixties was to get the violent oppression of black people on camera, remain passive, and let the world see how the powers that be deal with black men, women, and children who stand up for themselves. What a perversion for white supremacists to employ this approach when the cameras are on, to make black activists appear to be the violent and unreasonable ones, while continuing their brutality when the cameras are off. Lucky for us they lack the discipline to keep their violence clandestine. That, and the fact that we all have cameras in our pockets at all times, will make it hard for them to keep up the charade.

So, Dad, you were right, Innis was justified and seeing that Nazi getting choked was a delight, but I was also right. It didn't help our narrative, and ultimately everyone on that stage played into Geraldo's P. T. Barnumesque freak show.

UNCLE HAROLD VERSUS THE COPS

I complain about rampant police brutality a lot, as one should. Someone asked me, hadn't I ever had a GOOD experience with cops, so I posted this story to Facebook:

I ran out of gas going around a curve.

Luckily my VW bus kept rolling just enough for me to get to a safe pull-over spot, but I was on a red curb. I saw a group of cops eating pizza and I approached 'em.

"Hey, sorry to interrupt your dinner but I just ran out of gas. Can I go get some gas without getting a ticket?"

One cop said, "Yeah, sure. Give me just a minute and I'll give you a lift."

He then gulped his pizza, said good-bye to his buddies, and took me to the gas station. I got out of his car and realized I hadn't brought my wallet with me. Not a big deal; I was close to home and so I started walking.

The cop pulled up next to me: "Hey, I was gonna give you a ride back, where you going?" I explained that I had to go grab my wallet and he said, "Oh, it won't take more than a couple of bucks to fill that can. I got ya."

He then insisted I take the two bucks, and after I got my gas he drove me back to my bus. I told him that I was amazed by his kindness and he handed me his card, an awesome baseball card–type deal that Sac PD had at the time, and told me to let people know. We both knew what he meant by that, and I promised I would, and I did, and now I'm doing it again.

My Uncle Harold, a black man who grew up in the segregated South, wrote me the following email:

Nephew, I am having a difficult time trying to figure out what point you were making with this story.

I didn't want to ask you in front of people if it was a joke or you were trying to show that all Police are not bad and they do Help, Protect, and Serve the public? If it was the latter, I agree. I am certain there are some dedicated Police out there that do very humane things beyond what they are hired to do as in the case you expressed and later, the Lady in MI that the Cop took to Walmart and bought her a $50 child car seat. Such a nice story. I am certain that some people of color might have a similar story, but I am in my 70s and can't share a positive one with you. I have been shot at by the Police, taken to jail, fined for disorderly conduct simply because of my complexion of which I had no choice. I have many more deplorable stories to tell you.

I have heard the story of you stepping in front of an Officer that was planning to arrest a Black Man that was not doing anything wrong and telling them to arrest you, not him. I always enjoy hearing your dad telling me about that event. So much for that, tell me what's going on with this shit??????????????

It hurt to think of the jovial, intelligent, loving man being treated so awfully, though it wasn't news. Harold had worked hard to get a job with the post office so he could transfer out of the South, and, sadly, coming to California did not mean an end to his struggles with people who judged him by the color of his skin, including people in positions of power.

I assured him, promised him, that I knew this story was the exception not the rule, and that I saw what cops were actually doing out there, that my stories of their abuses outnumbered stories like this one 100 to 1.

My dad asked Harold about the email. Harold explained:

John, I wanted to know why Keith "Out of the Blue" without any reason and at a time when his Uncle's people are getting beat and shot by Police without provocation put that compliment to a COP on FACETIME.

And, I was pleased to see he added *I was satisfied with my favorite Nephew's response.*

I mostly included this story here so that my brothers know who Uncle Harold's favorite nephew is.

SHARPS

The SHARPS, Skinheads Against Racial Prejudice.

SHARPS were more than just skinheads trying to stick to the original values and tradition, they were ready to take on the racist skinheads who'd co-opted the movement.

I liked that SHARPS stood up to Nazi skins when nobody else would. I liked that they would use the Nazi skins' own tactics to let them know they were not welcome in our scene. In the end I don't know what worked, what drove the Nazis out, but I knew that trying to work with them, convert them, or ignore them failed miserably. The SHARPS at the very least evened up the score a bit.

At the same time, being honest, I usually wasn't very happy when SHARPS were present at a show. They were mostly super masculine guys who liked to fight, and if some misunderstanding happened you could end up at the receiving end of their boots. I always thought that they should make it a policy to only fight one-on-one if fighting anyone who wasn't a white supremacist, lest they become the cats that rid us of the rat problem, only to reward us with a cat problem. Of course, I never suggested this to them.

I had several friends who were SHARPS. One guy in particular, I'll call him Josh, told me he was trying to get the SHARPS to do positive things in the community, offering their services to remove graffiti from synagogues, or provide security at cultural events that Nazi skins might target. He was frustrated that he got no response from the other SHARPS. Years later he now has long dreadlocks and is a reggae DJ.

I remember going out to coffee with my roommate Chris. Chris is a black man, and he dressed like a goth. He was almost never without his leather jacket, "Christian Death" painted across the back. He had straightened hair and was thin and androgynously handsome. We reached the coffee shop. A group of SHARPS was hanging out. There were a few people of color who hung out with the SHARPS, but they were mostly white guys. Seeing a black dude their age come into the coffee shop, they all sat up. As Chris and I waited for our coffee, they came over one at a time to shake his hand and say hello, ask him how he was, and otherwise make a big show of being cool with him. I found it incredibly awkward.

As we headed back home, our caffeine needs satiated, I asked Chris about it. "Doesn't that bug the shit out of you?"

In his quiet voice Chris explained, "When it comes to skinheads, I much prefer them kissing my ass to kicking it."

I reminded Chris about the incident recently. He told me, "It was an awkward exchange. I remember that I thought it was disingenuous. But that was twenty-year-old me. Forty-six-year-old me just thinks we were kids trying to break barriers."

My little brother, James, had a less enjoyable run-in with one of these would-be superheroes. While attending a party at the apartment of a loudly and proudly gay friend of his, he heard a ruckus and saw one of the local SHARPS stomping out of the party onto the porch where James was hanging out with his friend Mel. The SHARP was calling people fags and poofs, and daring anyone to oppose him. Having come from a Southern California scene where people were much quicker to fight, James was amazed and disappointed that nobody seemed willing to stand up and take care of this guy, then he noticed his friend Mel reaching into his pocket for his gun. He pushed Mel's hand away from the pocket and told him, "I got this."

The skinhead continued taunting the invited guests at the party. When he stepped toward James, my brother took off his jacket and prepared to fight. The skin started walking quickly away, in the direction of The Weatherstone coffee shop, where more SHARPS would be hanging out. Worried that he was about to be faced with a whole group of SHARPS, James grabbed the guy, turned him around, and delivered a Swedish Kiss to his face. The Swedish Kiss, hitting someone in the face with the top of your head, was a favorite of my kid brother's since high school, despite me trying to talk him out of employing it. He followed up with three right hooks and put the guy on the ground.

One thing I've noted about all three of my brothers is their frightening ability to stay calm in a fight. James was on top of this skinhead, who was now crying and asking James to let him go. James told him, "Think next time before fucking with people," before getting off of him. The guy immediately ran off toward the coffee shop and James realized he might be in trouble. He went to Mel's house and called me.

I was at The Crest movie theater, emceeing the animation festival, when I was told there was a call for me in the office. I heard what happened and quickly started calling everyone and anyone I knew who had any association with the SHARPS. My roommate at the time, Todd, played trumpet for the ska band Filibuster, a favorite of the SHARPS. He helped me reach another member of the band, who I knew the SHARPS had great respect for.

"Hey man, James got into it with one of the SHARPS. Guy was drunk and making problems at a party. Can you help me make sure this is just between the two of them?" I was assured it wouldn't be a problem.

By the time I caught up with James he had blood dripping down his face. "I thought he didn't hit you?"

"He didn't."

"Why are you bleeding?"

His right hand went right to the source of the bleeding. He looked at his red fingers. "Goddammit. That's where my head connected with his teeth."

"Man, you gotta get that move out of your itinerary. You're gonna kill someone. For now you should get a tetanus shot."

A couple weeks later James walked into a bar and saw the guy hanging out with some other SHARPS. Dude's friends hopped off their bar stools and started at James, but dude put his hands on their chests and got them to sit down. He walked up to my brother and apologized. "I was being an asshole for far too long. I deserved it."

We heard he quit running with the SHARPS shortly thereafter.

I didn't like a lot of the SHARPS, and I loved several of them. I think of them like the jocks in high school, just a level of masculinity I have never related to, but the worst jocks in high school beat up geeky kids, and effeminate kids, and other easy targets. At least the SHARPS focused their violent tendencies on guys who were neither easy targets nor undeserving of a beating. Whatever other issues I may have had with them, I will always admire them for their Nazi punching. Well done, crew, well done.

RAIDER

Raider was my neighbor. Raider loved my band, which was good since we loudly rehearsed in my living room, just a few yards from his windows. He told me I sang like "the guy from Skynyrd." This brought me no end of teasing from my bandmates but I knew he meant it as the highest compliment he could muster. Raider got along well on our block. It was considered a "bad neighborhood," but like most bad neighborhoods I'd lived in, it wasn't so bad once you'd made friends with your neighbors. The man who lived downstairs from us constantly got robbed and vandalized. He actually grew suspicious of us, me, my brother James, and our roommate Allan, because our house never got messed with. I told him, "It might help that everyone here knows and likes us, and you're just a grumpy prick who calls the cops with noise complaints." This did nothing to alleviate his suspicions.

Raider had no problems in the neighborhood. He was the only white guy in a crew of dudes who played basketball every day in the park across from our flats. He drank beers with Alex, who lived downstairs from him. I took a couple of beers over and introduced myself to Alex. He was a polite, soft-spoken Mexican man who told me he couldn't come to our parties because there were too many pretty girls there and his girlfriend didn't like that. A week later my brother told me, "Good job befriending the most powerful drug dealer in the neighborhood. We are untouchable now."

"Alex?" I asked, surprised.

"Yeah man, Alex is an OG." I don't know if this was true, but as I said, we were treated alright.

Our parties were delightful chaos. My band would play sixties garage-inspired punk, our friends would come play music, and the guests would be a mix of Chicanos, and geeky punks, dudes in dresses, and everyone getting along. Even the cops who'd come by were cool. They never shut us down, and we always made sure we had the music turned low by 10:00 p.m. and everything else quiet by midnight.

Raider seemed to epitomize the vibe of this neighborhood. He was the only big, goofy, Southern-rock-loving redneck around, but he managed to fit in great just by being a nice guy.

Raider invited James into his flat. There James saw another side of our neighbor. He had a framed document on the wall titled "The Responsibilities of a Proud White Wife." It was a racist, misogynistic screed. Looking around, there were other white-pride emblems including a Confederate flag.

James told me all about it when he got back to our place. "Dude, Raider is a big ol' racist."

A few days later we noticed all of Raider's basketball buddies hanging on his porch. To our surprise they'd go in and out of the house to grab beers from the fridge.

I guess Raider saw white supremacy like he saw being a Raiders fan. He had his team, and he'd cheer them on, and if you were a Rams fan (like James) or black, like all of his friends, well, he'd keep the rivalry friendly. What I'm saying is, he never enforced his "Raiders Fan Parking Only" sign. I just couldn't quite wrap my head around this. Um, dude, your team has a really bad rap for violence and oppression, and I don't mean the Raiders, although . . . just nevermind. Nevermind. Your basketball pals seem to be dealing with you better than I ever could. Good luck, Raider.

HOW TO GET ALONG WITH WOMEN

My next book will be titled *How to Get Along with Women*.

It will be four hundred pages long.

The first page will read, "The same way you get along with men, now quit bein' an asshole."

This will be followed by 399 pages of *Lord of the Rings* haiku, just because I already have that written.

OUTSIDE OLD IRONSIDES

I was leaving Old Ironsides after a night of drinking. I was far from shitfaced but there was definitely a nice warmth in my chest and belly. The bar was closing for the night, so I'd have to find somewhere else to drink or give up and go home to bed.

A cop was parked right outside the door and I didn't think much of it. Probably just looking for drunks getting into cars, I figured, and I wasn't drivin' so all was fine with the world.

A black man, at least a decade my senior, was leaving just ahead of me. He was a dapper enough looking guy and the least drunk acting of the crowd. I stopped to button my coat and the cop approached the guy.

"Excuse me, do you have any ID on you?" the cop asked him.

"No, sorry. My wallet's at my buddy's place about two blocks from here. Is there a problem?"

"The law says you're supposed to have ID on you at all times. Do you live in town?"

I decided to stick around and witness what was happening here. "No, I live in the Bay Area, I'm here visiting my friend. The one who lives two blocks from here."

"No local address and no ID, that makes you a vagrant. I'm gonna have to take you in."

This cop was harassing and now arresting the only black man in sight while drunk white boys climbed behind steering wheels all around us.

Maybe I was drunker than I thought, because I heard myself yelling at the cop. "What the hell is this? You didn't ask nobody else for ID. I ain't got mine either."

"Stay out of this," the cop warned me.

"No this is bullshit"—and with that I was in his face. "You're gonna stand out here and wait for the first nonwhite face. What are you trying to keep downtown white? It's too late."

I was pushing closer and closer to him until finally he put his hand to my chest and gave a shove, landing me on my ass. The whole while the older black man stayed calm and polite, offering to be escorted to his friend's apartment where he could retrieve his ID and prove that he did indeed have a place to stay.

Faced with this polite black man and this mouthy little white boy yelling in his face, the cop still went about arresting the black guy, even after shoving me to the ground.

"Fuck you!" I hollered, getting up. I was determined to get arrested in this guy's place, or at least to get dragged in with him.

My friend Dave grabbed me and told the cop he'd get me out of there. "No! Fuck you, Dave. This is bullshit."

Dave pushed me halfway home. "Dude, what's wrong with you? That was messed-up shit. That cop was a racist asshole." I charged him as I finally gave up and started walking toward home on my own. I was ready for Dave to say that the dude might have fit a description, or to give me some other bullshit line to justify the cop's behavior.

"Yeah, and you getting that cop more angry was going to help the guy he was harassing?" he snapped back at me. "That guy was handling it much better than you were if you would have shut up and given him the chance. You did not help, hero."

Dave left me in my living room feeling powerless and clumsy.

CHARLIE CHAPLIN

I love silent comedies, and in particular the films of Charlie Chaplin. If you really want to appreciate Chaplin, to see the pathos and heart he put into his comedies, watch them with a kid. A kid will ask questions.

I was watching some Chaplin with a four-year-old and she asked, "Was Charlie a good guy or a bad guy?"

I said, "Um . . . I always assumed he was a good guy. Why do you ask?"

"He's always stealing food."

Damn. That's true. Dude would steal your hot dog right out of the bun. A regular wiener wrangler. It was a good question, I thought it deserved a real answer. I didn't want to insult her intelligence and dumb it down.

I told her, "Charlie steals because he's hungry. Everyone has to eat. It's not the same as stealing because you're greedy or lazy." I worried my answer was too complicated.

She said, "OK," and that was it. I felt like she got it. I was proud of her and proud of myself for not copping out.

A few minutes later she asked me, "Why are the police always so mean to Charlie?"

Wanting to give an equally honest answer I said, "Well, the thing is, cops are dicks."

She had to find out eventually, better she hear it from me than on the street.

Later in the film Charlie goes to jail. After all that hustling for food and a place to sleep he ends up in jail, and this is a foreign concept to the kid. How do I explain jail to a child?

"Well, the thing is, as a society we've decided that we're totally okay with housing and feeding people, but we insist they commit a crime first."

Many cities have made it a crime to be homeless. Personally, I'm okay with spending tax money on arresting people for being homeless. But let's not put them in regular jail with real criminals who are violent, or smoked pot. Let's have a special jail for them. I don't mean to go easy on them. This jail should have all the regular jail stuff, three hot meals and a cot to sleep in, a library, access to education and job training.

And then let's give them the keys to it . . . and maybe make it house-shaped.

FARTIE MCFUCKBUTT INTERVIEW

F artie McFuckButt is an old and dear friend of mine. I am respecting his wishes and not using his real name in this interview. I did not give him the opportunity to choose his own pseudonym.

Fartie McFuckButt is a legend to anyone who enjoys live music in Sacramento.

He's also been a favorite punching bag of Nazis over the years. Fartie's war stories have become part of our town's mythology. Wanting to hear them from the source, I reach out and he agrees to meet me at Coffee Works on Folsom. He is late, which I know to expect from a dude who always overbooks himself. It's a hot Sacramento spring day, so I grab a small cold brew coffee and wait for Fartie. In a corner of the coffee shop I spy Brian McKenna, another local show promoter. He's excited to hear what Fartie and I will be discussing. "Oh, man, I've punched some Nazis over the years," he says, relishing the memory.

Fartie shows up twenty minutes later and we grab a table. He is not the rail-thin young man he once was. He still sports a mop of thick, messy, black hair, but with a nice smattering of gray now joining the party. He manages to somehow stay right on the edge of unshaven, never quite reaching bearded.

I tell Fartie how I remember us meeting, describing him getting tired of me sneaking into his club and finally agreeing to let me in free in exchange for odd jobs.

He has no recollection of this but says it sounds like something he would do, and especially something he'd have done for me. He liked me, he explains, not just because I was friends with his girlfriend, but also because "You were a true-blue music fan and I thought you were someone who was for real."

When I was attending these shows in the late eighties and early nineties, white-power skinheads were a constant presence in the punk scene and at Fartie's "Tread Mark Club" (not its actual name) in particular. Fartie, having a few years on me, remembers it starting earlier, with racist skinheads showing up in Sacramento in the early eighties when he was booking punk shows featuring bands like Flipper, and the Dead Kennedys. He was surprised to see a macho, racist scene attach itself to punk of all things. "I would expect that more at like a Lynrd Skynyrd concert. Nothing against Lynyrd Skynyrd but I mean you know that just kind of white trash, white supremacist kind of thing, but there it was." The uniform was already in place, bald heads, white t-shirts or polo shirts, suspenders, tight Levi's with thin red suspenders, and of course they had their Doc Martens. "They really did have the look, it's who they were."

And they weren't just at his shows. Coming downtown, he remembers, meant you were likely to run into racist skinheads, hanging out on corners, or at the record store.

I ask Fartie something I've been wondering about since I was a teenager. How did these assholes keep getting into his shows? Why did he let them in?

"Well, you know, that's uh . . . that's just your whole First Amendment thing or whatever. That was me saying, the best I could . . . " He interrupts himself to say, defensively, "I want to make clear, too, I don't think we had that many fights inside. They mostly happened outside."

That's true, but the racist skinheads WERE inside.

Fartie describes his struggle with what to do, and it sounds like he harbored some sympathy for them, hoping that they were just dumb kids who were going to grow out of this idiotic phase. He didn't want the fights, but he did want to see if his shows might have some beneficial influence.

"They were brains that were forming poorly but they weren't formed yet. So I always felt like maybe there was some redemption. I wasn't trying to alienate anyone, I was trying to embrace everyone. And hope that that would appease things, and um . . . I know it sounds naive . . . "

I agree that it was naive, and simplistic of him. Of course, embracing a young Nazi kid who you can maybe influence toward a better way of thinking might be admirable, but how many black, gay, Jewish, female kids are you then robbing of that scene, that embrace, by allowing it to be full of people who intentionally make others unwelcome? Of course he was young then himself, and over time he'd pay dearly for this naiveté.

Eventually there was a list of people who were known troublemakers, not to be allowed in, and of course there were many skinheads on the list.

Fartie continued to struggle with the antiracist skinheads and punks coming to fight the racists. At one point he canceled a show by Filibuster (a much-loved local ska band). "I love all those guys, but I was pissed off because it was like 'I host you guys here! You play here! Don't show up in a pickup truck because you heard there were some skinheads here you want to start a fight with.'"

This makes me love Filibuster even more than I already did. I ask Fartie about SHARPS, explaining that I didn't like them at the time, but now looking back I wonder, did they help solve the Nazi problem?

His feeling is that they only worsened the problem. "You know what, they were just dudes who wanted to fight. They cloaked it in some kind of ideal but they were just dudes who wanted to fight."

I come from a family that loves fighting, and it got me in trouble, and it hurt people, which wasn't the part I liked. My brother became a professional fighter. He was a dude who liked to fight, and he found a socially acceptable, consensual, hell, even productive way to do it. I wondered, if these SHARPS were just dudes who liked to fight, why not go fight Nazis? That's admirable, right?

Fartie has a different perspective on this. "When I set up an all-ages rock and roll show and they show up to fight, I don't think that was anywhere on the flyer, you guys, I don't think I advertised that on the poster. I did not invite you here to fight. So at that point they've crossed a line, a public line of decorum, but they've crossed me at that point, too." After a pause he continues, "We were just talking about the Ariana Grande thing . . . "

Fartie and I are having this chat just days after twenty-two people, mostly kids, died in a bomb blast at an Ariana Grande concert in Manchester, England. "That kinda thing just kills me, as it's always killed me. There's nothing I hated more than anyone ever getting hurt at one of my shows, under any circumstances. I don't care if they fell down and cut their knee open. I always hated it. I didn't like mosh pits at my shows."

"I DID!" I tell him, with a laugh.

Skinheads were not the only concern when it came to the safety of his audience at punk shows, with slam dancing, stage diving, and many of us showing up after engaging in a bit of underage drinking or other substance consumption. He once worried he'd be losing his business to a lawyer whose daughter got hurt when a stage diver landed on her.

The security charged with keeping us wild kids in check was a bunch of older black dudes, one of whom, Lincoln, I got chummy with even though he once hit me with a flashlight.

"Lincoln, why'd you hit me?"

Lincoln answered, "You're doing that stupid dancing. I didn't want you to get hurt."

"Lincoln, the only time I ever got hurt dancing was just now when you hit me."

"Just behave yourself," he said, patting me on the back.

Fartie tells me he went through several different groups of security guards, including one guy who was a champion kickboxer. "It's like, well, that's nice you can do that, I don't want to see any of that here."

The kickboxer's brother was a racist skinhead.

When Fartie ran into skinheads around town, they knew him as the dude who put on the punk shows. "They'd go, 'hey, Fartie,' and I would very reluctantly go [in a deep, low voice], 'hey, guys.' You know, um, I wasn't like 'fuck you, racist!' but, I like to lead by example and I feel like that's the best thing I could do was be better."

I asked him more about the decision process when it came to letting people in, or not letting people in. What about blatantly racist things, swastika patches or tattoos, that kind of thing?

"Oh, no no no no, you know I don't think I noticed that. I don't think anybody came in with a big swastika. Maybe people had swastika tattoos that I didn't notice because they weren't coming in shirtless . . ."

I recall they often ended up that way in the pit.

Fartie recalls something that would be very hard to explain to anyone outside of the punk scene, regarding the hateful symbol in the days before racist punk became a thing. "The swastika thing with punk rock was such a weird thing." Sid Vicious of the Sex Pistols wore a swastika around his neck. Other punks did this, as well.

I totally get his hesitancy here, and it being awkward to try to explain out of context. I never wore a swastika, I wouldn't, but I too was a Sid Vicious fan, and I had, at one time, defended his wearing the swastika. I think this is a great example of a lot of us white kids thinking we're being rebellious and not being able to see these things from other contexts. Sure, our white parents and grandparents hated that symbol and so it was ripe for pissing them off, but what about our Jewish friends and their grandparents? To them, more white people running around with swastikas on might not seem so rebellious, just a terrible status quo.

Fartie jokes, "And honest to God that is a cool symbol. It's one of the coolest symbols ever, for crying out loud. Fucking Nazis get to have that? [In a comical voice] *Say what you will about Nazis, they had a sense of design and image.* It felt more cartoonish, at first. Now I think anybody who sports that is a freakin' idiot."

So, after his optimism and generosity toward the kids with the shaved heads who were fucking up his shows, I wonder how did he come to be on the receiving end of their boots and was it Nazi skins or SHARPS?

"It was Nazis. There were so many incidents."

Fartie recounted an infamous night in Sacramento's history, from his perspective.

In the early morning hours of January 4, 1992, a group of nine black men and women entered the Carrows Restaurant in midtown. As they entered, a table of skinheads got up and left. A short time later a car full of men drove by firing guns into the restaurant. No one was hit.

The rumor around town was that the shots were actually aimed at a group of SHARPS who was also at Carrows and had nothing to do with the group of black people there but I've never heard this confirmed.

Fartie tells of going into Carrows, as he often did in the a.m. hours after shows, shortly before the attack. Two skinheads sitting at a table recognized him and said hello. He said a hushed hello back and went to his own table.

He noticed the table of young black kids seated by the window, right across from him. "Maybe they'd been out dancing that night or something, they were dressed really nice, you know . . . just teenagers hanging out."

He didn't get the news of what happened until the following Monday and called an anonymous tip line to report that he'd seen two skinheads there earlier in the evening.

He didn't know their names, only their nicknames, and he stressed that he was not saying they had anything to do with the shooting, but he thought they might have information.

He had called anonymously and had not left any personal information. Much to his surprise, ten minutes later local police along with the FBI showed up at Fartie's door. It turned out the

133

waitress had tipped them off that Fartie had been there and that the skinheads had said hi to him.

He told the cops the same thing he'd already told the anonymous tip line, and apparently word got out.

"Next thing I know I got guys walking up to me at shows saying, 'You're dead,' and like, 'You ratted these guys out.'"

Promoting his shows with posters and handbills became difficult and dangerous. Fartie describes having to run every time he saw a group of skinheads, and they tended to hang out at all the places he needed to be at to distribute his flyers, at shows, parties, and even at dance clubs, where they'd hang out in the parking lot.

Skinheads had an odd relationship with scenes they claimed to hate; lacking any real scene of their own, they'd hang out near dance clubs, go to mod dance parties, presumably just to make trouble, making fun of the clothes and the scooters, calling the guys gay and harassing the girls with lewd comments, trying to provoke fights.

Fartie had several close calls when he had to jump into a friend's van and race away with threats and beer bottles hurled after them.

Of course, as a show promoter, Fartie couldn't hide. "I was so easy to find that it led to my beating a few times. You know, it's like, 'He's at the club. When he's not at the club he goes to Carrows or Lyon's, so we'll beat him in the parking lot of Lyon's.'"

The skinhead who said hi to Fartie on the night of the shooting was the brother of Fartie's kickboxing security guy. He sat down with his employee and explained that he hadn't thrown anyone under the bus. That he didn't say they had done it. And, luckily, surprisingly that worked and things calmed down, for a while.

He didn't always get off that easy. On another occasion, seeing a group of Nazi skinheads run out of the club, he followed them into the parking lot, foolishly neglecting to alert his security team. "I thought that sticking a shot glass in my pocket would be all I needed to go out and confront five or six skinheads," he laughs.

He tried to be tactful, asking them if there was a problem, if anyone was messing with them. As he talked, they formed a circle around him, and he knew he was in trouble. "They make a move on me and I grab my shot glass. And I just BOOM nail a guy on the head with it. It was Curly from The Three Stooges comedy here. I hit him on the head with the shot glass 'boop' and the shot glass goes wooooooo smash and breaks in the parking lot about twenty feet away. That was the extent of my damage on them."

Decades later Fartie and I are able to laugh as he describes his head being bounced back and forth between cars, and we laugh harder as he remembers that they tried to break a bottle over his head but couldn't get it to shatter. It doesn't work like in the movies, he explains. "It's like 'Clink,' 'Clink,' 'Clink.' They hit me over the head about ten times and the bottle never broke."

After taking a few punches to the face, he wrestled away from them, and not having another shot glass to bounce off of their skulls, he starts to spit blood at them. "My fighting back gesture was to spit my own blood on them. 'Fuck you guys, ptoo ptoo ptoo' Ha ha ha, that was the best I could do at that point."

Eventually he got back into the club, and security raced to the parking lot, but the skinheads had made their escape by then.

An incident that's harder to find the humor in took place in 1996 and put Fartie in the hospital with a broken back. He'd taken a break from doing shows at The Tread Mark Club and restarted his monthly newspaper *The Shitburg Times* (not it's actual name). He booked a one-off show in the middle of trying to get the second issue of the paper out. The bands, Pocket Change and Welt, were good friends of his, and he was looking forward to a fun and uneventful night.

During the show, Fartie hid out in the DJ booth with his ancient laptop working on the paper. He had only a few days to make their deadline and prove to sponsors he could successfully get the paper out on a monthly basis.

He heard from security that they'd thrown some skinheads out for starting fights on the dance floor. "Oh man, I don't do a show for months, I come back and this is what happens."

The show ended and the sound man was loading equipment out to his truck, leaving the doors to the club open. Fartie's in the club, holding his computer as a carload of skinheads walk in, five or six of 'em, plus their girlfriends. "With their stupid bowl cuts. I hated that look, that costume of thuggery, that costume of racism, all of it, all the ugliness that was tied into it, that was that look. That's what they were trying to tell me with that look. That was a look that they deliberately donned because that's how they were identifying."

The skins didn't recognize Fartie. "Who are you?"

"Oh, I'm just cleaning up."

"Who else is here?"

Fartie's friends Katy and Megan were closing up the bar and the soundman was outside loading equipment into his truck. Security had gone home already.

"Oh, well, security is squaring up with the owner in the office and we're just loading out sound." Fartie tried not to reveal that he was the producer behind the show.

"And the whole time I'm just looking around, 'Did Eric leave a mic stand in here, anything that I can, is there a chair, anything that I can grab to defend myself?'"

Fartie was also aware that he was holding a laptop with the whole next issue of his newspaper saved on it. He tells them, "Hang on a minute, guys," and walks over to the stage where he carefully sets his computer down. "I walk back up to them and I'm like, 'I don't know if there's anything else I can help you . . .' and they just jump me. But all I can think at that point is, 'Thank God I set my computer down.'"

The skinheads all joined in kicking Fartie with their steel-toe boots, and punching him. "I'm swinging like a madman, I'm trying to clock a jaw or a nose if I can. But I'm also doing whatever I can to cover my face." He describes not feeling fear, just anger, and even a sense of familiarity. "I just wanna jump up and punch somebody if I can. I've had this happen before, where I literally know the routine. So, after it was over and they go running out the door, I'm laying there and I can feel sand and grit on my tongue, and I know it's teeth."

He jumped to his feet to go get their license plate number, assuming the adrenaline's gonna kick in and help him through the pain, as it's done in the past.

But as soon as Fartie got up, he knew this time was different. Screaming pain cut right through him and put him back on the ground. An ambulance was called and he spent the next ten days in the hospital.

Fartie laughs remembering how frustrated he'd get that, in all the times he'd had his face beaten in, nobody ever thinks to take a picture of the carnage for him. I recall that the story around town was that they'd broken his cheekbone and his eye had popped out of his head.

"That did not happen. They're just confusing my lazy eye."

What did happen was that he fractured the three lower vertebrae of his back. After his ten-day hospital stay, with no health insurance, he had to wear a tight back brace and utilize a wheelchair some friends managed to find for him. "Which is fine except I lived up a flight of stairs." His friends brought his computer to the hospital, and he managed to give them verbal instructions there in the hospital room. Amazingly, the paper came out on time.

I commended him on his brilliant move, saving the computer.

"Yeah. Faces heal, computers don't."

Nobody was arrested over the beating. "I was shown mugshots of skinheads, but guess what. They all look alike."

Some believe the lead guy was Dave Lynch, a notorious white supremacist and organizer for the American Front who was later murdered in his own home in Rocklin, California, a suburb of Sacramento.

Pressing Fartie again on his earlier assertion that SHARPS and Nazis were two sides of the same coin, I had to ask him, "How many times did skinheads jump you?"

"Three times."

"Were you ever jumped by SHARPS?"

"No. No, that never happened, to their credit."

BYE, BYE, BEN

I wrote my nephew to tell him I couldn't be his friend on Facebook anymore. I love him, of course, but his pro-Trump posts stank of xenophobia and sexism, and, as I explained to him, it hurt to see my nephew behaving like one of Hitler's brown shirts. He was surprised, but accepting, and because he grew up with the same vicious sense of humor I did, he gave one hell of a zinger as he said good-bye: "If it makes you feel better, I do thank you for making my news feed great again."

Losing that regular connection to a family member stung, a lot, but like most people, I'd gotten used to losing friends on a daily basis as the alt-right both lent Trump their support and used his rise to advance their own. I've lost "friends" who I'd never interacted with other than on social media, and I've lost friends whose casual racism they kept to themselves, or at least hidden from me, until it became less casual once they had an actual dog in the hunt and were feeling threatened, and encouraged. (I was going to make a joke about casual racism being racism in polo shirts and khakis, but then that's exactly the uniform the alt-right Sieg Heilers adopted for their latest marches.)

I know some of you feel driven to hang onto the racist friends as you try to convert them. Let them go or keep working on them but don't fucking defend them and their racism! I've seen people who would sooner let go their aversion to racial profiling than let go of Sam Harris because they were so flattered when he "hearted" their reply to his tweet once. Let him go. Bye, bye, Sam.

I'm not saying it's easy. Here is a eulogy to one very close friendship of mine that ended shortly after Donald Trump was elected.

I met Ben in summer school between our freshman and sophomore years of high school. He complimented my David Bowie t-shirt.

It had been ten months, and one whole school year, since I'd moved to the Sacramento area from Corona and I still hadn't managed to make any friends. My Southern California fashion sense meant that I was a weirdo, but not quite the right kind of weirdo to get along with the weird kids. The cheese stands alone.

But here, this goofy kid who always wore Hawaiian shirts had complimented my David Bowie shirt. This was promising. I desperately wanted him to be my friend.

"You like Bowie?" I asked.

"Yeah, I have a bunch of his tapes."

This was enough to build a friendship off of but we were in the last week of summer school. I had to move quick. In the fall Ben would go back to Roseville High, and I, having already been kicked out of Roseville, would be returning to Success Continuation High School.

I waited until the last bell rang on the last day of summer school. I was as nervous as I'd have been asking a girl out on a date. Doing my best to sound cool but with a tremor in my voice,

I asked, "Hey man, *Labyrinth* with David Bowie is on cable tonight. You wanna come check it out? We have a pool."

I ad-libbed the bit about the pool and immediately worried it sounded too desperate.

"Yeah."

Yeah? Yeah was the answer I'd hoped for. I explained where I lived and he laughed because he lived just a few blocks away.

Ben rode his bike over and we swam, and had dinner with my folks, and swam some more. And then Ben asked if I smoked pot. I told him I didn't, worrying this would be the end of the friendship, and wondering if maybe this should be the end of the friendship. He said he wanted to smoke a quick bowl and did so in my parents' downstairs bathroom, blowing the smoke up into the ceiling fan. I didn't like this at all, knowing my dad would freak about drugs being done in his house, but damn it, I really needed a friend. I decided to overlook this minor quirk.

After watching *Labyrinth,* Ben called his folks and asked if he could spend the night. They said okay, and my mom drove us to rent a pile of horror movies from the local video rental place.

We hung out watching splatter flicks and talking about music all the next day. I was incredibly amused that my parents liked him so much and thought he was such a nice kid. He was nice, but not in the way parents mean when they say someone is a nice kid. Not only did Ben do any drug available to him, he sold individually rolled joints for a dollar each at school, and he had an extensive collection of cassette tapes, most of which he stole from unlocked cars during his early morning paper route. There was something almost magical about such an eclectic music collection. Listening to music was my hobby, and I put a lot of effort into it. I was proud of the wide range my own collection covered.

And here Ben had gotten to a similar point by mixing and matching whatever his neighbors forgot to securely lock up.

Ben's parents came by to meet my folks. His mom, Betty, was a sweet woman with enormous breasts and his dad was an absolute maniac. George mentioned his wife's "knockers" at least once per conversation, kept pictures of her in her Halloween Elvira costume on him at all times (an actual hard copy photograph, at the ready in his wallet, these being the dark ages before cell phones). He was overly friendly and pushy.

"You guys gotten to know the neighborhood yet?" he asked my dad. "There's a Kentucky Fried Chicken right up on Douglas. Just right there. You like KFC? It's probably the best fast food. Get a big bucket, with some corn and mashed potatoes and gravy, you got yourself a proper dinner, you know? Have you guys been up there yet, to the KFC?"

My dad changed the subject a few times, but George always found a way to bring it back to the Colonel's delicious fried chicken, and though it could have gone either way, Dad seemed to decide that George was one of those characters he'd be amused by instead of annoyed by. He played along, "Um, George, would you like to stay for dinner? We can get some Kentucky Fried Chicken."

"That's a great idea!"

And George of course made no move to pay for it. After all, we had a pool.

The next weekend it was my turn to visit Ben at home. George and Betty, I discovered, rarely left the bedroom. Ben told me his parents were nymphomaniacs and, they didn't know he knew this, also swingers. I wondered if they'd invite my folks to partner swap with 'em.

"No, man. They have a club they go to. There are dances."

"You think they'll invite my parents to go to their club dances?"

"Probably not."

I wondered what was wrong with my parents.

We watched music documentaries, and more horror movies, and checked out Ben's collection of porn magazines. He also had porn novels, something I'd never been exposed to before. They all seemed to involve incest, father/daughter, mother/daughter, brother/sister.

"Dude, this is some weird shit!"

Besides the nymphomania, which at fifteen years of age, I thought seemed like maybe the best psychological disorder you could hope for in a spouse, there were other signs that things were a little off in George's world. The house was very dark, with all the blinds pulled at all times. George had a recliner that sat centered in front of the television. Anyone who wanted to watch TV with him would have to sit on the couch and turn their head sideways, or pull up a chair from the dining room table.

George was over-the-top chipper and affectionate until he got mad, and then he was explosive. I remember me and my friend Christian coming to visit Ben, and he was out running an errand. While we waited, we helped Betty bring some groceries in from the van, and George tore open a huge package of artificial crab. We got a live infomercial for the reassembled white fish with red dye added.

"You guys ever try this artificial crab? It's the best. Betty, don't bother with dinner, I'm just gonna finish off this artificial crab." As he shoveled it into his mouth in huge handfuls right from the Styrofoam tray, Christian and I looked at each other and didn't dare laugh.

"You boys sure you don't want some? So good!" It was weird for us to see an adult acting like this, but also kind of nice to see a man so thoroughly enjoying something, even if that something was a small step up from flavored Styrofoam.

I loved going to see movies with Ben and his folks, always mindless comedies. Jim Varney's *Ernest* movies cracked them up, and they would roar with infectious, contagious laughter, which I thought was just wonderful.

When George wasn't laughing at Ernest asking Vern if he knew what he meant, or singing the praises of imitation crab, he was constantly kicking me out of his house, his truck, his van. He caught Ben and me smoking when picking us up from school one day. He'd come from a different direction than we'd expected, and we were caught unaware. We both dropped our cigarettes and casually stomped them out, hoping he hadn't noticed. It was clear right away that he had as we climbed into the cab of his truck under his angry glare. We rode in silence for a few minutes, as he was too angry to speak, and then, "Really, Ben? You want to smoke cigarettes? Look, if you want to kill yourself don't let me stop you. Why don't we just make it quicker? How about we go home I'll give you my shotgun and you can shoot yourself in the face three times? How does that sound?"

From the backseat of the king cab, I said, softly, "Um . . . Mr. Bradley, it would be pretty hard to shoot yourself in the face more than once."

He pulled the truck over. "OUT!" and I walked the rest of the way home.

If he'd known what else Ben smoked, he'd have lost his mind. Most of our parents in the late eighties were still in the full grip of drug war hysteria. Marijuana, not yet the miracle cure for all that ails ya, was a "stepping stone drug," it would make you crazy, etc. And Ben's father, who'd gotten through the sixties without ever trying weed, was the worst. I can't trust anyone who was a young

144

person in the sixties and didn't try weed at least. When I asked George if he liked The Beatles, figuring this was always a safe bonding place, he answered, "Oh, you mean the band that ruined rock and roll with their goddamn drugs? No, I do not." It was then that I knew how I felt about George. Fuck this guy forever.

And yet, Ben's house was where the kids went to drink, smoke, do drugs, and watch porn. Obviously it wasn't the house with the laid-back parents, that was Jacob's house. Jacob's mom would let you do any drugs that weren't white, so long as you brought enough to share. She was on an antidrug crusade as much as the other parents, she was just more particular about which drugs. You might have a room full of kids sitting around tripping on acid that she had supplied, listening to her horror stories of the government putting some kind of tracking device in crank.

Let's face it, though, kids will do drugs. Maybe giving them honest, if somewhat paranoid, advice about which drugs are RE-ALLY bad isn't such a crazy idea. The little nanobots hidden in your drugs will crawl through your pores and report your location to the helicopters overhead if you accidentally do the government's tweek—well, okay, that *was* a pretty crazy idea.

Ben's dad, on the other hand, seemed the most likely to shoot you for doing drugs in his house, and he had the guns, but other than that minor detail, his house was a perfect teenage drug den, mostly on account of George being employed as a firefighter, working forty-eight-hour shifts at the firehouse. Add in the sex addiction, and Ben's mom was often at the fire department as well, taking care of things in the parking lot. They had a great "bedroom on wheels"–style van that they put to good and frequent use.

And, when Ben's parents weren't keeping the van a rockin' while on the clock at the Fire Department, he and his mate were doing up the swingers' scene. This left an empty house much of the time, and since George was also a doomsday prepper, he kept the place unbelievably well stocked with munchies. He'd never been in the military, or hunted, or done anything to give him any idea how being a survivalist was supposed to work, so instead of freeze-dried goods, beans, and firewood, he had an extra restaurant-size freezer and a refrigerator in the garage in addition to a full one in the house. When the bombs fell, Ben's family would have all the postapocalypse frozen pizza bagels they'd need, so long as power stayed on. In the meanwhile, stoned kids watching dirty movies didn't have to venture out to 7-11, where they were likely to run into their own parents or the overenthusiastic local cops.

As I've said, Ben never met an intoxicant he didn't like. When traditional highs were not available, my friend was a bold adventurer, ingesting household cleaners, smoking various vegetables, and keeping notes. He was the kid who found out which aerosols granted the good highs, and which ones made your friends ponder whether to call 911, or do a drive-by drop-off at the emergency room. VCR head cleaner, by the way, will give you a ride you wouldn't believe, just one of the many exciting discoveries made in Doctor Ben's laboratory.

On a typical evening at Ben's, we were chowing down chocolate chip granola bars and the ever-popular frozen pizzas. There was nothing worth watching on cable and so Ben was persuaded to grab the video tapes out of his parents' closet. These were unlabeled tapes full of porn. I didn't know where they came from, but I imagined the swinger folks swapped and traded tapes they had dubbed. Why this household had no originals from which to dub I couldn't figure, but it wouldn't be hard to believe that George would be the cheapskate who took, but never left, a penny from the "Take a penny, Leave a penny" dish down at the 7-11.

Ben popped in the first flick and we all focused like we never did in prealgebra, but it was pretty amateur. Hairy and nasty and all-around uncomfortable to look at. Boos and pizza crusts were hurled at the screen as Ben inhaled something he claimed was jet fuel. He buzzed his way to the VCR, hit the eject button, and barely managed to pop in tape number two.

As Ben took another deep inhale, his parents appeared on screen. Ben must not have registered this fact too quickly because he just stood frozen as his dad pounded his mom from behind while she chewed on the most insanely sized dildo I'd ever seen. It got worse. George began chanting, "I'm gonna put it in the butt, I'm gonna put it in the butt!" to Betty's playful return chant of, "No, No, not in the butt. Not in the butt."

Well, he did put it in the butt, and Ben's mom decided that despite her repeated pleas of "No, No, Not in the butt. Not in the butt" being ignored, being in the butt was indeed a good thing. As she yelled, "YES! YES!" I felt like screaming, "NO MEANS NO, GEORGE!" It wasn't easy being a porn-loving feminist teenager watching his friend's parents not respecting sexual boundaries.

I pondered what their safe word might be, as Ben suddenly registered what was happening and lurched forward, pushing the eject button on the VCR hard enough to send the entire machine spinning off the top of the television and onto the floor. The tape went off, but not before we all heard his mom start singing a little song along the lines of "I love it, I love it, I love it in the butt."

I could've sat there in shock for quite some time, but instead I had to jump into action, as our clueless friend Mike began berating Ben. "What the fuck, dude! Why'd you turn off the fuckin' video. Dude, he was totally giving it to her in the ass. And THAT BITCH WAS LOVING IT!"

I barked at Mike to shut up and told Ben to go outside. He grabbed his jet fuel and his cigarettes and headed out to the driveway without a word. I turned on Mike, "What's wrong with you, man? Those were Ben's fuckin' parents!" being more literal than intended.

"George and Betty?! Bullshit, dude. That wasn't his folks." Mike knew Ben's folks. Mike had lived two houses from Ben's folks all his life. How the hell could Mike not be able to tell that these were Ben's parents?

I made a decision then, and I'd like to believe that my motivation was pure. Ben was still outside, and I turned to Mike. "I'm gonna put this back on for just a second. You look good. Then you shut your goddamn mouth about it forever." I popped the evil video tape back in, and Mike and I both squinted at the screen.

"Dude, that is so hot. And so not Ben's parents," he moaned.

"Mike. Look at the bed. Look at the blankets. Look at the big ass painting of a lion with a mane like an Afro on the wall! Now come here." I led him to Ben's parents' room. There it was. The bed. The blankets. The bigass painting of the lion with an Afro. I took a chance and moved a pillow. There it was. The mondo plastic phallus, with chew marks. "Now Mike, will you shut up?!"

"Dude! Oh my God. . . . Let me have that tape. I can't believe Ben's mom loves it in the ass. You've got to let me take that tape." He must have seen the hatred in my eyes as he took a few steps back, but he just got more desperate. "C'mon man, you don't understand, I really have to have that tape. I have had the hots for Betty all my life."

"Mike. You're gonna go home now or I'm going to beat the shit out of you. If you talk to Ben, one word, I'm going to beat the shit out of you. If you do anything other than walk out that door

I'm going to beat the shit out of you." I didn't usually act like a bully, but sometimes a guy needs the threat of having the shit beaten out of him.

"Dude. I can't go home, I'm high! I'll be cool, man. Don't make me go home." And with this, Mike started to cry.

"Okay, shut up. I don't care where you go. I'm not gonna call your house and check on you, I just need you out of here."

"Dude! There's nowhere else to go, man. I'm high, dude. You can't kick me out, man." The tears were really flowing.

"Alright, Mike. Go to the back bedroom and go to sleep or something."

"Thanks, dude. Thanks. Really, man, I'm too high to go anywhere else, man. I'll just go to sleep." And as Mike turned to go to the back room, I punched him. I hit him as hard as I could on the back of his right shoulder, causing him to drop Ben's parents' sex tape that he'd stashed in his sweatshirt.

I ushered him into the back bedroom, with him crying all the way. "Everytime I see you I'm going to hit you, so don't let me see you," I threatened as I shut the door.

I had no idea what to say to Ben. I found him sitting on the driveway. He didn't look too bad off. He'd been dealing with nympho parents for years, I guess. Hell, I'd known them for less than a year and I'd already gotten used to his mom answering the phone while having sex.

"Hi, is Ben there?"

"Um, yes, but, oooh, ah, I can't get him right now!" making me an unwitting part of their sex.

"Okay. Why don't you hang up and then let me call back and DON'T ANSWER THE PHONE?!"

"Oh, Oh, Oh, Okay."

"Thanks. Tell George I said 'Hi!'"

I couldn't help but wonder if maybe Ben was, at least partially, just going through the motions because this was supposed to be upsetting. I mean, Ben would like to appear as a normal guy, and normal guys get weirded out about seeing their parents fucking. Ben was probably pretty confused and not sure how to feel. It was a bizarre situation to say the least, and of course he had all the jet fuel swimming around in his brain.

"You okay, dude?" I asked.

He didn't look at me as he answered. "Yeah. I'm alright." He flicked his cigarette down the driveway. We went inside and watched *Return of the Dead*.

Ben's other friends were surprised that I had made it to the ripe old age of fifteen without ever smoking pot. Many afternoons I'd sit in George's recliner enjoying his many cable channels and eating up his apocalypse snacks while he fought fires or had sex with his wife in a parking lot, and his son smoked pot with his other buddies in the garage.

Amusingly, all of my friends' parents worried about me. The only teetotaler in the bunch, and they were sure that I was on drugs. "Is Keith . . . okay?" they'd ask. "Is there anything you want to tell us?"

On one idyllic spring day, I was watching an Echo and the Bunnymen documentary, and drinking Coke in a can while sitting in George's recliner. All that was missing was pizza and it would have been a perfect situation. I headed out to the garage freezer to get some. Ben and his buddies were in a circle and I noticed an odd contraption in the center. They had cut the bottom off of a two-liter bottle, then set it in a pitcher of water. They put a small metal bowl with a stem at the top of the bottle, and as they pulled the bottle up out of the water, air was forced through the bowl, which they'd packed full of marijuana and were now holding a lighter to. The bottle would fill up with smoke, which, once cooled, they'd suck down into their lungs, lowering the bottle to push the smoke in faster.

"Whoa. Nature abhors a vacuum!"

They all turned to stare at me. "You guys have created an artificial lung!" I was excited and explained to them how their gravity bong, as I learned it was called, employed the principles they'd failed to understand in science class. Ben looked up at me with bloodshot eyes. "You want a hit?"

I did. For some reason it was this DIY ingenuity that finally brought me around to giving weed a try. I took a nice big hit.

People who smoke weed love getting someone high for the first time. If you want to score a few free tokes, just tell people you don't smoke pot. Even now, as someone who used to but doesn't anymore, I have friends champing at the bit to smoke out with me. Ben and his circle of stoners watched me eagerly, waiting for some sign of my being high.

"You feelin' it, man?"

"You high?"

"I don't think I am. I'm not feeling anything." I answered.

"Well you gotta give it a minute."

I gave it many minutes. I hypothesized that because I was hyperactive maybe weed didn't hit me like it hit them. I explained that Ritalin would be like speed to them but not to me. They asked me for some Ritalin.

Eventually they got bored of watching me not be high so we put everything away, sprayed some air freshener, and headed on our bikes toward Denio's Farmers' Market and Auction, a local flea market.

I pedaled up next to Ben. "Hey, is this the best day you've ever had in your life?"

He looked at me. "Dude, you're high."

"Well . . . " I answered, thinking it over. "Maybe. But maybe not. I mean, it could be the weed but it could be that it just actually is a great day. Is it not gorgeous out? Could it just be that the sky really is terrifically blue today, that a nice breeze is blowing, and that we're with our best friends riding our bikes? I mean, that's a pretty great day, yes?"

"Dude, you're high as fuck."

I still wasn't sure I was. I wasn't really sure that I'd gotten high until the next morning when I woke up and looked at the t-shirts I'd purchased from the flea market. The first had Spuds Mac-Kenzie, the Budweiser party dug, flattened as roadkill having just been run over by a Coors truck.

The next had Mickey Mouse's dog, Pluto, shaking between two fire hydrants with "Decisions, Decisions" written above.

The third featured a French fry, an old wavy one like you'd get at the drive-in snack bar. A caterpillar with thick glasses was mounting the wavy French fry, and lines were drawn to indicate motion in his hips. The caterpillar was fucking the wavy French fry. Above the wavy French fry was a word bubble. The wavy French fry was saying to the bespectacled caterpillar, "Get off of me, you asshole, I'm a French fry."

Yeah, I was high.

It's amazing in hindsight that Ben's drug consumption stayed hidden from his folks for as long as it did. Eventually, though, he got busted at school. He was caught with some weed, and the principal told him his little spoon necklace tested positive for meth residue. He confessed to the meth. I told him later that I was pretty sure they hadn't tested his necklace. They just knew what a tiny spoon pendant means, as did everyone else in the world except for Ben's parents.

Ben's home life, already pretty surreal, became a nightmare of tough love combined with mental instability. When his dad wasn't screaming at him and hitting him, he was hugging him and assuring him he loved him. He often threatened Ben with kicking him out of the house until Ben tried to call his bluff, packing a bag and heading to our house, where my mom said he could, with his parents' permission, stay as long as he needed.

Ben and I were standing on the driveway when his dad pulled up. "Ben, get the fuck in the truck."

"No," he answered, staring at his feet. George grabbed him and threw him on the ground, kicking him twice in the stomach.

"Get the fuck off him." George looked up to see that my brother Edward was standing over him ready to brain him with a shovel. "Now!"

He got back in his truck. "Ben, get in." Ben got in.

Things got worse when Ben's mom caught him drinking and, no doubt emotionally exhausted and terrified herself, tried to hide it from George, to spare them all from his overwrought response. George found out anyway. I was at their house, once again helping Ben pack a bag, when I heard the answering machine pick up, and George leaving a message in a deep growl. "Betty, Ben, get out of my house. When I get home, if you are there, I will shoot you. Anything of yours that is left in the house, I will burn." I suggested to both of them that they call the police immediately.

Ben stayed with us for a couple of days. If I remember correctly, Betty stayed with some friends. A week later they were back in the house and things were back to their version of normal.

George came to school to pick Ben up unexpectedly and caught him wearing eyeliner. He smacked his son in the face in front of everyone. Ben decided to come out bisexual to his dad in the truck. That went about as well as could be expected.

Sometime later George walked in on Ben having sex with a girl in his room. "Good boy," was all he said.

This cycle of angry explosions and smothering love went on for years. After turning eighteen, Ben moved out, went to jail, moved back in. I went to visit Ben at his parents' place after we'd both turned twenty-one. I had a few beers from the case we bought. Ben drank the rest and was very careful to get the cans into the outside trash, no evidence of his drinking left in the house.

George checked the trash upon arriving home from a dance party, finding the cans. Ben told him the beers were mine, and that it was okay for me to drink because I didn't have a problem. George was remarkably calm and told me that I needed to not drink around Ben if I wanted to be a good friend to him. I agreed and made a promise to myself never to visit that house again.

George was invited to resign from the fire department after driving the big hook and ladder truck home from work in a fit of rage and chasing Ben down the street with a shotgun. Other than having more time for sex and swinger parties now, things continued on pretty much as usual. Ben continued to live there.

He was in and out of jail, mostly short stays, nothing major. At one point he did a couple months in, and upon getting out he raced to an old girlfriend's house and banged on her door. When she opened he said, "Quick! I haven't had sex in four months!" We both had a good laugh together over this line actually working.

Ben started dating a girl with white-power tattoos. He told me her last boyfriend was a skinhead and that she didn't feel that way herself. I wouldn't hang out with them as long as the tats were visible, and they remained visible. Ben and I were already moving apart and this accelerated it. Ben took it hard when they broke up, going on another bender and burning an A, her first initial, into his arm with cigarettes.

We saw each other only occasionally as we entered our twenties and had several fallings-out, including me threatening to call the police if he got in his truck and tried to drive after showing up at my place already drunk and proceeding to slam more beers, but we always made up. He came to my wedding and bragged to my teetotaler mom that he was a changed man, meaning that he had arranged a sober ride home before getting smashed on wedding wine.

He did in fact seem to be doing well. He was married and had a steady job. He and his wife were able to buy a house from her aunt, getting a really good deal.

Like many old friends, we got back in touch more regularly via Facebook. Ben started leaning more toward his dad's conservative politics, but a few times when I called him out on the cruelty of his positions and the rude combative way he chose to express them, or on his lack of sympathy for people with the same struggles he had faced, he'd write me and apologize. He specifically mentioned his father and not wanting to be like him.

I was curious and checked out George's Facebook page. It was full of pictures of very young-looking Asian girls and links to what seemed to be sex trade tourism sites. He was very thin, and I suspected his health was not good. Ben confirmed, his father had cancer. When George died, Ben eulogized him, "I couldn't have asked for a better father." I thought, *Yes, you could have. You deserved better.* I didn't know if it was crueler to say this or not to say this. I expressed my condolences.

I got a few more angry screeds and then a few more apologies, but eventually the apologies stopped while the screeds continued and escalated. The more power the alt-right gained, the more frustrating Ben parroting their talking points, sharing their easily debunked fake news, and otherwise cheering them on became. I

155

noticed his friends list filling up with people more extreme than him as he steadily moved in their direction. Finally, Trump took the White House and moved Steve Bannon into it. Ben, like a lot of other folks, was a closet Trump supporter. He'd slam Hillary and then say, "I'm not supporting either party," but he was gleeful over Trump's win and over the prospect that he'd make good on his promise to "lock her up."

Again I engaged with him, but with this victory for his alt-right views came a new level of smugness and a more public embrace of alt-right ideals. Ben didn't need any sympathy or understanding now. He himself was doing good. He'd gotten his, and everyone else would have to get their own, like he did, or die trying.

I decided it was time to say good-bye to George's son, Ben. I'll always be sad thinking about the good times we shared, and about the horrific upbringing my friend suffered through, but saying good-bye to him wasn't difficult. By that point he'd been, for years, behaving more like George and less like the sweet, goofy kid who complimented my David Bowie shirt.

SAFE SPACES

I hear that safe spaces are for young people who are so afraid of hearing other's opinions that they shut down discourse and debate.

Um, no. There is no more debate needed with bigots. Bigotry deserves no more respect, consideration, or debate than alchemy or phrenology or any other archaic, thoroughly debunked idea. Bigots derail actual discussions. Nobody should have to constantly pause in a debate to defend their worth as a human being. I think maybe we could be more honest, maybe change the name from Safe Spaces to No Being-an-Asshole Spaces.

Also, one doesn't exist solely in safe spaces. Can't a person get a break and a breather from a world that's hostile to them? Why is that a problem? So no break? Engagement with bigots all the time in all spaces even for the greatly outnumbered victims of the bigotry?

It's so weird to me that people complain so much about young people having safe spaces, a place for a temporary reprieve and rest from bigotry, but I don't hear any fuss about rich people continuing to live in gated communities. People live behind a gate, safe from us poor folks. They get in their air-conditioned cars, radios turned to Christian radio, or conservative talk radio, or maybe some classic rock as they drive to a private parking lot of a private club or well-secured upscale shopping center, and some kid taking public transportation and walking the streets can't have a rest in a café or bookstore where it's understood that bigotry isn't welcome?

Punch yourself in the face.

FIFTEEN DOLLARS

Minimum wage is shit, and if you want a person who clocks in and works forty hours a week to not make enough to get by, then you're a shit person. If you think they don't earn a proper living and respect, then I suspect you've never done their job.

I've done it, and it's awful. I earned every penny of that three dollars and seventy five cents per hour.

You're getting a hamburger for a dollar. It's made of meat from a living thing that had to be born and raised and killed and slaughtered and shipped and cooked, and put on a bun made of wheat that was planted and watered and grown and harvested and milled and combined with yet more ingredients and shaped and baked, and topped with things that were planted and grown and harvested and shipped and sliced, and you order it from a person whose life is really fucking hard and it's your fault and then you'll complain that he wasn't pleasant enough, cheerful enough to be serving you, and on top of that you don't think they deserve to make enough money to pay rent, and buy groceries, and definitely not enough to have something extra to invest in the future, spend on getting an education, or put down on a car or a house? Shit person.

Fifteen-dollar living wage, for anyone working a job.

But I try to be flexible. I try to meet people halfway, so here's an alternate plan.

How about in lieu of a living wage, every customer service person gets to choose one customer a day and punch them in the face. I think that would go a long way to improving the experience. And at the end of the week, if they didn't punch anyone in the face, a small bag of heroin to use or sell.

I PLEDGE ALLEGIANCE

olin Kaepernick, I'll remind you because our news cycles move fast and our attention span is ever-shrinking or perhaps just stretched to the point of breaking, was a quarterback with the San Francisco 49ers who chose not to stand for the National Anthem, causing much outrage, thoughts for the children, and clutching of pearls.

And Kaepernick, of course, pissed me off. Not the protest, just that now, because of him, I know something about sports. I'd made it this far in life, and now suddenly I know a player's name, team, and even his position. I don't totally know what a quarterback does, but I know that Kaepernick is one. His protest I'm fine with. Why wouldn't I be? He chose not to express patriotism that he did not feel. And seeing this man not feeling patriotic, what a strange response on the part of America; "Fake it!" That's what we told him. "You're not feeling love of country? Well, fake it. Stand there and act like you're feeling good about this country, we don't want to hear your complaints."

I hope those of us telling him to fake it don't have this attitude with our romantic partners, too. "What's that? You didn't cum?

Well, fake it." That isn't fair. We shouldn't ask someone to fake it for us. I mean, not all the time. Once in a while is okay, on your birthday for sure, but she or he deserves a real orgasm, and goddammit, America, so does Colin Kaepernick. Don't ask him to stand up there, "Oh yes, America, you're so good. Oh America, you're the biggest country I've ever had."

Of course, as a cisgendered, heterosexual, white male, I related to Kaepernick and his struggle. [Sarcasm.] I too once had to struggle with being asked to perform an act of patriotism that I did not agree with.

I had excitedly enrolled in band in junior high. Surprise! On the first day of class I took my seat along with a dozen or so other socially awkward kids on metal folding chairs in front of Mr. Haney. To my surprise, he asked us to rise for the Pledge of Allegiance.

This was Southern California in the eighties. I don't know how it was elsewhere, but we hadn't been made to say the pledge in class since first memorizing it in the early years of grade school, and I wasn't real sure I wanted to pledge my allegiance. It wasn't that I didn't feel patriotic. I did. I didn't stop feeling patriotic until November 2016. It was just that pledging your allegiance was a bit of a heavy commitment for a thirteen-year-old. "Whoa, America, slow down. I think I might just like you as a friend. I think we should see other countries first." I stood up, respectfully, along with my fellow aspiring band geeks, but instead of placing my hand over my heart, I kept both of mine at my sides and my mouth shut. "I pledge allegiance to the flag of the United States of . . . "

"Stop! Stop!" Mr. Haney waved his hands. "One student is not saying it." He didn't single me out by name, but he may as well have, there was no mystery as to who was the troublemaker in this group. "Start again from the beginning."

Some dirty looks were beamed my way as, with a chorus of sighs, the ritual started again. "I pledge allegiance, to the flag . . ." I continued to stand silently, hands at my side.

"Stop! Everyone sit down."

All eyes were angrily on me as we again took our seats and Mr. Haney decided to give us a heartfelt talk. He explained that, like *LOL* many men his age, he'd been to Germany. He wasn't involved in the war, he just toured there some years later with a jazz trio. With a sincere and gentle tone he told us of his visit to a café along the Berlin Wall. For my younger readers, there used to be a wall in Germany separating it into two countries, Pink Floyd was there, things got crazy. He was able to see, from the balcony of this West German coffee shop, into East Germany, where, he explained, they didn't have the freedoms that American kids took for granted, and as a result it was a lifeless, dreary, gray place.

I raised my hand. "Yes, Keith," he called on me, full of patience and hope.

"Mr. Haney, I was just wondering, on what side of that wall do *nice* you think they were more likely to coerce children into pledging their allegiance?"

And *that* is the story of why I do not know how to play the clarinet.

A couple of years ago I went to see my friend Nick graduate from high school. The audience rose to their feet to recite the Pledge of Allegiance. I did as I usually do and politely stood in silence as everyone around me pledged their allegiance to a flag. A woman in the front row had a nice strong voice and was proudly taking a leadership role in the recitation. She then raised her voice even louder, to a yell, a roar even, as she reached the most contentious phrase, ". . . one nation UNDER GOD!!!" and she looked around

chud

163

just daring any motherfucker to come at her. I smiled and then actually let an out-loud laugh escape as she smugly uttered the next word "indivisible" with no indication of irony whatsoever.

TEN REASONS WHY YOUR RAPE JOKE ISN'T WORKING, BRO

10. Liberal left-wing agenda.
9. Too many pussy-whipped dudes in the crowd with their wives or girlfriends.
8. ABC's *The View*.
7. You didn't yell the punchline loud enough.
6. You didn't repeat the word "rape" enough times.
5. They hate your freedom.
4. Feminists have no sense of humor.
3. The audience is frightened (and kind of excited) by your house arrest anklet.
2. Too believable. You're coming off too rapey. Some say the best way to fix this is not to tell rape jokes. This is what's known as The Rape Joke Paradox.
1. You're too nice.

Also, Obama and Hillary probably have something to do with it, but you knew that.

GOOD-LOOKING SANTAS

Check out my "Not a Racist" punch card! I got it by having a black friend. Every time I do something that isn't racist I get a punch, and every ten punches I get to say the n-word!

I don't say the n-word and I'm not even gonna write it here. I don't care for the n-word, though, by which I mean the phrase *the n-word*, as there is something infantile about it.

I have three stories about personal experiences I've had with the word this phrase describes, and I wanted to tell them without saying the n-word or *the n-word*.

I went to my friends and asked for their thoughts on this dilemma. Several friends who are black said, "Just say it." But at least one black friend said, "Nah. I think you shouldn't use it," and I told him I wouldn't. My joke that's not a joke is that I'll say it when 100 percent of black people tell me it's okay for me to say it.

Predictably, a white comedian friend of mine got bent out of shape at this.

"For fuck's sake, it's just a word and your intent is clear," he charged.

I answered him, "I want black people to come to my comedy shows too, and so I don't want to make them uncomfortable."

"We're comedians. Isn't it our job to make people uncomfortable?"

"I consider it my job to make comfortable people uncomfortable, but when it comes to black people in my audience, I figure they've already been made uncomfortable enough times by people who look like me. I'm aimin' to give them the night off."

I burn through online "friends" pretty quick.

Another comedian friend, Kareem Daniels (yes, a black guy; I'm sure there is a white Kareem out there somewhere, but this Kareem isn't him), was doing a set on a show I produced and he asked me if HE could say the n-word. I told him it felt weird for a dude named Kareem to be asking me for permission to say the n-word, and to go right ahead.

Back to my problem, I had these three stories. They were honest, and they were mine, and I wanted to find a creative way to tell them. That's when I came across my friend Nat Towsen's "The Hidden Language of" column for *Vice* magazine. While exploring the hidden language of department store Santas, Towsen discovered a graceful solution to a problem they had, that I decided might be applied to my problem, as well.

Black families would come in for their picture with Santa, of course, and often they'd want a Santa who was also black. Bigger department stores kept just such a Santa around, but the problem was how to call him to service. Yelling, "Hey Barney, send out the black guy!" is troublesome. "Special Santa" wasn't going to work either, as special has picked up all manner of connotations over the years. The solution they came up with was to call for "the good-looking Santa." What jolly black Father Christmas is gonna complain about that? What black family is going to object to their Santa being "the good-looking Santa"?

If it's good enough for Christmas, it's good enough for me. So here are three true stories about a horrible word. When I say Good-looking Santa in these stories, you'll know the actual word that was said. Sorry about that.

NO GOOD-LOOKING SANTAS ALLOWED

My older brother, Henry, and I were playing in our backyard. Henry loved to piss people off. It's a power that even a kid can wield: say a word and watch people lose their minds, incredibly satisfying for a child, or dudes on Reddit. I myself used to love to get dressed up in church clothes, and when old ladies would bend over to admire me, I'd say "fucking dick shit titty" and watch their faces sour before they walked quickly away. They'd give my mother dirty looks and I knew I could count on them to never explain why.

On this beautiful spring day we were positioning my *Star Wars* figures for an epic battle. We had the hose ready. There were often floods in our battles.

Henry looked up and saw a big 1970s Afro showing over the top of our brick wall. It was Dwayne, one of only a handful of black kids in our neighborhood at that time. I followed Henry's gaze and then hopped up to go say hi to our buddy Dwayne, who was closer to Henry's age, ahead of me by four or five years.

Henry tells me, "Let him know, there are no good-looking Santas allowed in our yard."

I didn't know what a good-looking Santa was, but I figured Henry had a good a reason for not wanting them in. I ran to deliver the message.

"Hey, Dwayne!" I called out as I jumped up on some boxes and peered over the wall.

"Hey, Keith. What are you up to?" he answered.

"Just playing *Star Wars*. Hey, there're no good-looking Santas allowed in our backyard."

Dwayne stared at me, and he must have seen innocence or cluelessness. "Is that so? Tell me, little man, is Henry back there with you?"

"Yep."

"I thought so. Hey, can I come back?"

"Sure!" I answered as I swung the gate open for Dwayne, who ran and grabbed Henry before my brother was able to make it through the backdoor and into the safety of our house. Dwayne threw Henry down, got on top of him, and started punching.

Confused, I headed into the house, where my mom was hosting a PTA meeting. A PTA meeting in Corona, California, was an ethnically diverse affair. I approached my mom, and, standing in the middle of a living room full of Mexican ladies, white ladies, a Hawaiian woman married to a black man, and at least one Samoan, I asked, "Mom, what's a good-looking Santa?"

The room fell silent, all eyes on Mom to see how she'd handle this. Mom was cool. She looked at my dopey face, and like Dwayne, she knew right away that I had no idea what I was saying.

"That is an awful word, designed to hurt black people. You wouldn't want Lonnie, or Richie, or Dwayne to hear you say that and feel bad, would you?"

"No." I answered, staring at my feet.

Embarrassed and mad, I walked back into the backyard and sat down and watched Dwayne jump up and down on my brother's head.

Note: I have four brothers. None of them are named Henry. One of them will be glad I didn't use his real name, and three of them will be kind of pissed.

THE OLD MAN WHO LOVED MOVIES

I was doing some shows in Vancouver, Canada, and staying at The Dufferin Hotel. The Dufferin was in a funky old building and the ground floor featured a gay bar and a restaurant that made a decent falafel, and, when you were too broke to order anything but toast and coffee, brought you peanut butter, allowing you to still get a decent meal out of it.

I was initially put on the second floor, where sleep was impossible, as men were partying in every room, chasing one another up and down the hallways. I opened my door and a man in nothing but boxer shorts stopped to say hello.

"Um . . . is this party gonna go on much longer?" I asked, groggily.

"Oh! I think maybe you don't want to be on the second floor," was his confusing answer.

I don't like to complain when people are having fun on a Friday night, but a couple hours later it was time to get some sleep. I called downstairs. "Hi, I'm in room 203. It's really loud up here. Can I move to another floor by chance?"

"You didn't want to be on the second floor? Oh my god, I'm sorry."

I didn't know that I looked like that much of a party boy, but I was flattered by the assumption. I explained that, no, I wasn't there for the second-floor shenanigans as fun as they seemed to be, I actually wanted to get some sleep. I grabbed my backpack and was delivered to a room on the fourth floor, where I slept like a log, missing all the fun.

Even though comedy keeps me up late, I'm not good at sleeping in. Most mornings I'd grab some coffee and toast (with peanut butter!) and then head out to see Vancouver. In the afternoon I'd watch a movie or two.

So, gay bar, free peanut butter, a whole floor devoted to dude parties, this seemed like a veritable bastion of happy, fun liberalism, the kind of place where I'm comfortable, where I fit.

I became friends with Rod, a senior citizen who spent most of his time sitting in The Dufferin's lobby. Rod watched as many movies as I did and we bonded over discussing the latest films.

"You seen that new Cronenberg film?" he asked.

"*Crash?* Yeah, I saw it yesterday. It's garbage. It's on a very small list of movies I've walked out on. I wanted to make it to the end but the damn thing just droned on and on."

"Yes. Garbage! Absolutely. Pretentious, mindless, garbage," Rod replied.

I think it was here that we bonded. Rod and I continued to discuss movies, sometimes over coffee and toast, with peanut butter.

My run in Vancouver came to an end, and I was heading through the lobby with my backpack all loaded, on my way to a very long drive home. I said good-bye to Rod, told him I'd really enjoyed meeting him. As I opened the front door to leave, he called after me.

"Be careful out there. Lots of good-looking Santas out today."

I stopped in shock. My face went pale, which probably made Rod more comfortable. I didn't know what to say. Rod couldn't be a horrible racist, he had good taste in movies. He knew Cronenberg's *Crash* was garbage.

This is where I discovered how invisible racism and racists can be to white people. They're not always sporting white-power tattoos, sometimes they don't even have goatees, or hipster Hitler haircuts. Sometimes they're the sweet old dude who discusses movies with you in the lobby of the gay-friendly hotel.

Rod knew why I was awestruck. Rather than walk it back, he doubled down. "I'm staying in. There are good-looking Santas everywhere today."

I was frozen with no idea how to respond, but feeling a need to do so. I heard my mouth reply, "That's OK, Rod, I like 'em," and I walked out the door.

"You like 'em?" I chastised myself as I navigated the busy sidewalk. But, as I thought about it later, this may have been a perfect response. I wasn't gonna change this old man's mind by getting mad at him, or telling him to piss off. But a nice, friendly "I like 'em" might just make him think. It's unlikely but it could happen. He might say, "Hmmm, Keith likes 'em, maybe they're alright. After all, he knew that Cronenberg's *Crash* was garbage."

A DOG NAMED SANTA

My little brother James is a goddamn sweetheart and sometimes it pisses me off.

We were living together in a flat in Sacramento shortly after he turned eighteen. One day he showed up with an adorably ugly, seemingly untrainable dog.

"What the hell, James? You can't have a dog. You ain't figured out how to take care of yourself yet," I berated him. He told me the story.

An old homeless woman was feeding the pup beer and rotten milk by the dumpster next to our place. James told her, "Hey, you can't feed a dog that shit."

"Fuck you. It's my dog, I'll feed him whatever the fuck I want. If he's your dog, you feed him, asshole," she snapped back.

"Fine, it's my dog then. Give him to me."

"You want him, you give me five dollars, fuckwad!"

"Fine! Here's five dollars!" and that's how my bleeding-heart, softy brother became a dog father. "What's his name?" he called after the woman as she hurried away with his money, before he had a chance to change his mind.

"Indo!" she shouted back. Indo was popular slang for a strong strain of weed.

Indo was a pain in the ass. Indo tore up pillows, shit in the house, and had no idea how to walk on a leash. He was also a snuggler and I fell in love with him, mostly because it was James who had to pick up after him, not me.

James took Indo across the street for a walk in the park and the squirrelly maniac dog got off his leash and bolted, not trying to get away, but running in big circles loving his freedom and taunting James hoping to play chase.

James called him again and again. "INDO! INDO! Come, now!"

Two black kids walked up to James. "Hey mister, what are you doing?"

"I'm calling my dog. He won't come back."

"That dog?" one of them asked, pointing.

"Yeah, that dog."

"That dog used to be our dog. His name ain't Indo."

"Well, what's his name?"

"His name is Santa." Notice, dear reader, the abbreviated, more casual version of good-looking Santa, with no hard Gs.

"Santa? I can't stand in this park yelling Santa!"

The kids laughed hard, and then called the dog over by the name he actually answered to and helped James get a leash on him. Unfortunately they had no interest in changing Santa's status from *used to be theirs* back to *theirs*, and they left my brother holding the leash.

James carried his dog upstairs to our pad, and I saw his distraught face. "What's up, dude?"

Looking like he was working hard to contain tears, he sputtered, "My dog's name is Santa!"

A few weeks later our friend Caroline, much better with dogs than us, agreed to adopt Santa. She renamed him JoJo the Dog-Faced Boy, taught him how to behave, sort of, and loved him to his dying day.

IS ERIC GAY?

The following is an actual phone conversation that took place between me and my landlord in the early 1990s.

"Hello."

It was Matt, the landlord, calling and he didn't have time for such small talk.

"Keith, Matt. I gotta ask you something. Is your roommate gay?"

"Yeah, Matt. Eric is gay."

Nobody who'd actually met Eric would have to ask this. Eric wasn't gay in any subtle kind of way. He would eventually make his way to that gay mecca, San Francisco, where he'd find his place as a much-loved drag performer working under the name Porsche 666. For now, he lived with us in an old Victorian that my former employer, Matt, owned. Eric's room was full of candles, silk scarves, and too much absinthe being consumed for me to be comfortable with these fire hazards.

Eric had once had his rent paid for him when a man he didn't really know but who was a regular at the coffee shop where Eric worked dropped an envelope on the counter addressed to him. Inside were a few crisp hundred dollar bills and a note saying, "I know times are tough and I want to help any way that I can. Us Nelly Queens have to stick together."

I was delighted at the idea of a Nelly Queen support network, and more so at Eric's description of the man as his Fairy Godmother.

Matt was only a little surprised at my confirming that I had a gay roommate living in the five-bedroom house he rented to me and a group of my friends. This brusque New Yorker thought of me, his young friend and former employee, as a typical California liberal, who he hoped would someday grow up, make some money, and join the Republican Party. "Why do you wanna live with a gay guy?" he asked.

"I like the swishy way he always pays his rent on time." I answered.

"Very funny. The guys next door said that he was on your back porch looking at their dicks."

Next door to us was a frat house, also owned by Matt. It always amused me that he thought these wealthy young conservatives had their heads on better than I did, even as they completely trashed the beautiful house he rented them, driving staples and nails into the carefully restored wood ceiling beams and walls when they had a "cave party," or managing to somehow lose the very expensive, and heavy, antique claw-foot bathtub from the upstairs bathroom, or making a habit of peeing together in a group off their back porch.

"He was looking at their dicks, eh? Well, we can't have that. You don't just go around looking at people's dicks. I'll definitely look into that for you, boss."

"Please do. That's not okay."

"I agree, Matt, one hundred percent, not okay at all. One quick question, though; what were their dicks doing out, exposed, on the back porch?"

I enjoyed the silence.

"Matt, could you look into that for me?" I continued.

"Make sure the rent check is in on time." And with a click, Matt ended this conversation definitively, never to revive it again.

THE HAPPIEST PLACE ON EARTH

When I see two dudes walking through Disneyland holding hands, I do the right thing, I leave 'em alone. I just let 'em be gay at Disneyland in peace.

I know that they're being brave, and I know that they get shit from horrible people just for being themselves, and what I WANT to do is run up to them and say, "Hey! I for one, am totally cool with you being gay! I think it's great! Here, be gay in front of my daughter. I don't mind. I love it. Look honey, see the nice gay guys? Aren't they great!"

I know this would be inappropriate, though, and I know it would get tedious having your Magic Kingdom experience interrupted repeatedly so you could help straight dudes address their hetero guilt, but would it also be kind of awesome? On some level? Maybe?

Couldn't there be something like what sports fans have? When my kid brother sees a Dodgers cap or a Rams jersey, he comments on it and has this instant, almost tribal camaraderie. I guess I just hit on why we liberals love bumper stickers so much, but then we feel guilty for driving. I could wear a rainbow flag t-shirt but that's false advertising and being a tease (because we all know what I got going on is HOT!), and those "Straight but not narrow t-shirts" just seem a bit too close to saying, "HEY EVERYBODY, I'M NOT GAY! Not that there's anything wrong with that."

So, um, anyway, dudes holding hands at Disneyland, I hope you had a good time. Also, you HELLA cut in front of us in line for It's a Small World. Not cool.

GRANDMA

I was sitting at the dinner table at my dad's house when completely out of the blue my grandma says to me, "You think black people are so great."

Say what you will, that woman knew how to start a conversation.

"What are you talking about, Grandma?"

"You think black people are so wonderful, why are most of the people in prison black?"

"Great question, Grandma. I'm sure it has nothing to do with them still living in the racist system that enslaved their grandparents, and that continues to oppress them in myriad ways."

"Oh, I'm so tired of hearing about slavery."

"Yeah, that must be hard for you."

We went on like this for a minute, threatening to derail another peaceful Jensen family dinner, not an unusual occurrence at all. My dad interrupted.

"Mom! Mom!" he cut her off midrant. "Which came first, the chicken or the egg?"

She looked at him incredulously, like he was the biggest idiot she'd ever met and then she answered him with a heavy tone of exasperation at being asked such an obvious question. "The chicken."

Dad looked at me, eyebrows raised, and I got his point. She was ambiguity aversion personified. The world was simple, and easy to understand, and she got it, and idiots like me did not.

I went back to enjoying my dinner.

KATHY GRIFFIN CUTS TRUMP'S HEAD OFF

Stand-up comedian Kathy Griffin posed for a photoshoot where she appeared to be holding Donald Trump's bloody, severed head, and many of the same people who ran out to buy "Cop Killer" by Ice-T and Body Count, who go see Doug Stanhope whenever he's in town, who love gangster rap and punk rock are jumping to decry her horrible act of simulated violence.

It was delightful to see friends who'd posted such favorites as "I hope Trump does win! It'll bring the revolution quicker!" just a year later crying, "Kathy Griffin went too far!"

I like to picture them wearing their favorite Cannibal Corpse t-shirt and listening to The Dead Kennedys' "Kill the Poor," which they know every word to, as they type out their bold condemnation of this stand-up comedian.

"The extreme left is just like the far right," I read in the headlines of several opinion pieces. And I agree. The alt-right white supremacists kill people, and the far-left comedians make cartoonish jokes about killing people. Exactly the same.

I read about how this was just like the people who I personally decried posting pictures of Obama being lynched. I wish it were the case, which is to say I wish that there were a history in America of selfish billionaires who sell our lives and livelihoods to the highest bidder getting their heads cut off. I also wish that there weren't a history full of black people being lynched. The best I can offer people making this complaint is that we warm up the guillotine and provide just such a scenario for future generations.

Normally when a comedian is being raked over the coals for something they've said, I don't jump to their defense and I don't see their freedom of speech as being threatened. In Griffin's case, a major network dropping her from their New Year's Eve show isn't a threat to her freedom of speech. What she did was punk as fuck, and punk as fuck doesn't get to do a major cable network's New Year's Eve show. I'm good with that. If she wants to be that badass, she may need to court a different fan base, and different channels to access them.

But the barrage of death threats, and threats of violence unleashed when Donald Trump tweets disdainfully, are a threat to her freedom of speech. Of course he has a right to reply to such a picture, but he also has a responsibility to know—and by now certainly ought to know—that he has a troll army eager to do his bidding.

Chuck Jones, president of United Steelworkers Local 1999, had the nerve to call Trump out in the media for grossly exaggerating how many jobs were saved by the agreement the President had "negotiated" (he gave them money) with United Technologies. The threats and harassment came almost immediately, but once our great leader tweeted that Jones did "a terrible job" representing workers, the abuse kicked up in frequency and ferocity including messages from people eager to let him know that they knew he had children. Donald Trump knows full well what he's doing when he targets someone on Twitter.

With Griffin, Donald kicked it up a notch by giving us the ridiculous story that little Barron Trump saw the image on the Internet and thought it was really his father. I'd be upset if my child saw such a horrifying image, and "fans" have indeed created some disturbing images of me. But my child doesn't see horrifying images on the Internet because my child is supervised while accessing the Internet because the Internet is where horrifying images live.

You'd think the Trumps of all parents would keep their little one away from the World Wide Web; after all, you wouldn't want the impressionable little scamp coming across footage of his dad talking about his sister's nice legs and breasts, or bragging about grabbing women by the pussy.

And why does the media get a pass for showing the image again, and again, and again, while condemning it? THEY showed it to impressionable children if anyone did. Kathy Griffin shared it only with people who subscribe to her social media accounts. The Disney Channel set hardly seems her demographic. Does little Barron follow Kathy Griffin on Instagram? That seems like a bad idea.

I have been targeted for attack via photographic simulated violence, but it was done so much less artfully than in Griffin's Trump pics. A meme of me making fun of libertarianism started making the rounds again, years after I'd initially told the joke featured in it. In the joke I describe my daughter not wanting to follow rules and instructions, as she wanted to be free, and I reply by teasing her that, like her, I just want to be free, so I wasn't going to obey traffic signs.

She reaches the realization that some rules need to be followed, and I joke that at the age of four, she'd been talked out of libertarianism. I told the joke only a couple of times, certainly not one of my greatest hits, but the meme keeps coming back around. Libertarian author and podcaster Tom Woods wrote about it, accusing me of child abuse, and his Twitter badasses came to call with a night of Twitter mobbing. Sadly, the best they could offer were poorly done Photoshop images of me with my neck cut open, blood spraying everywhere, or with dicks aimed at my face, shit that wasn't even worth forwarding to my followers. I'd love to have it done as well as Griffin and photographer Tyler Shields did it. I doubt I could afford them, although Griffin's price tag may have recently come down a bit.

I have no issue with Griffin. She did what a comedian should be doing and if she went a little too far, I'm good with that, too. We take those risks. Holy shit, some of the things I've said at open mic nights over the years! She apologized, let's move on. If you want to see much better references to separating the heads of greedy bastards from their bodies, I highly recommend you give "The Guillotine" by Oakland, California, hip-hop outfit The Coup a listen. They will not be apologizing or hosting New Year's Eve for a major cable network anytime soon.

KNOCK KNOCK

Knock! Knock!
    Who's there?
    Alex Jones.
  Alex Jones who?

Really? You're just gonna buy the lamestream media story that there was a knock on the door? They want you to believe someone knocked. The government wants you to believe someone knocked. Why did several news outlets originally report a ding-dong noise? And what about the peephole? Wouldn't the homeowner have just looked through the peephole? Immediately after the alleged knock there were reports of a second "knocker" that have just disappeared, not to be talked about after the first ten minutes of the story breaking. What happened to this second knocker? Did this story not fit the official narrative? Did anyone examine the supposed knockers' knuckles? The neighbors to the right and left didn't hear knocking. The town where the knocking occurred is a doorbell manufacturing town AND most of the homes have screen doors. If you add up the knocks it equals two. September 11th, people! Eleven looks like the roman numeral II.

If you don't see the Illuminati in this you're not looking hard enough. And why does SpellCheck capitalize Illuminati? Microsoft is so in on this. Our country's security systems are run on Microsoft. That terrify you? It should! Take off the blinders and put down the Kool-Aid, they'll be "knocking" on your door next!!! WILL YOU ANSWER?!

"Trump supporters really don't like it when you call them Nazis. Which is why I call them Nazis. Finally, an n-word that bothers white racists."

—Cate Gary, Trumpslayer

CATE GARY: TRUMPSLAYER

O ne of the things I love most about comedian Cate Gary is how much she gleefully fits the right's caricature of a lefty. Reading snarky tweets about us liberals and our radical lifestyle choices, I feel downright boring, sober, pajama-wearing hetero married to another white person that I am. Oh that for even a weekend my life could be half as exciting and scintillating as talk radio hosts and YouTube "experts" imagine it to be. While I know for a fact Cate and her partner also spend plenty of boring nights together watching TV, they are, on paper at least, exactly the right-wing nightmare of what us evil liberals would like to enforce as the mandatory new normal.

Just imagine the talk jock getting excited to the point of yelling (they'll apologize afterward, dear listeners, as if it doesn't happen at least once per show) describing Ms. Gary's home life. "This 'comedienne' billing herself as *The Trumpslayer*, lives in California, of course she does, and she works in tech, surprise. She's in a relationship with another woman, but she didn't used to be. She didn't leave her husband or boyfriend for her lesbian lover, oh no, her lover left their own gender! Her partner Robin Tran used to go by Robert. I'll let that sink in. Robin realized she was Robin a couple of years ago. And they parade this! They hold this up as something to be proud of with their 'comedy' show *Unconventional Lesbians*. Robin indeed jokes about telling her hardworking, immigrant parents that she was transgender. She jokes about this, people!"

I love it. And Cate and Robin love it. They do indeed tour their show *Unconventional Lesbians* and tell their story, hilariously and proudly. I asked Cate to tell me more about taking her and Robin's relationship to the stage.

They met in the open mic comedy scene where they were both young stand-up comedians struggling to find stage time and develop their comedic voice. "When we originally went out, we were just two open micers in love in what we presumed was a heterosexual relationship." The couple were still new when Robin began to transition, and, much to her relief, Cate didn't seem to think it was much of a big deal for their relationship. "We're both comedians; our first thought was 'Hey, why don't we try to make this into a stage show?' because we have no shame!"

Despite the self-effacing tone, Cate did see a real value in her and Robin's tale. Having heard many weepy tales of couples torn apart by transgenderism, they were excited to have a happier story to tell. And the response has been great, with profiles being done by *Pacific Standard* magazine, and *OC Weekly*, as well as a short documentary about Robin called *Tran*.

Their shows have also been well attended. People are curious, enthusiastic, and Cate says, "We're both really fucking funny."

Part of what makes their story so interesting is how little impact Robin's transition seemed to have on their relationship and their life together. Cate is candid and graphic describing how little impact it had on their sex life. "That's the big hang-up people have, like 'Oh the dick was really important with our fucking' and we weren't even using it," she says, laughing.

Facebook fans saw Robin going on her first exhilarating shopping trips to buy dresses, blouses, and skirts, usually with Cate, who does not dress particularly femme herself, coming along for the assist. And there was the pronoun shift. Once again, Cate didn't see a problem. "I'm like a grammar nerd, so that was just a fun exercise to me."

I imagine Robin nervous all day prepping for a really heavy, difficult coming-out conversation, and Cate responding with "You're trans? YES! I gotta call my agent. This is fucking gold!"

Cate laughs at this and considers what a boring stage show it would be if they were just an interracial, hetero couple.

With this background, nobody will be surprised to hear that Cate Gary is not a Trump supporter, but she has earned herself a reputation even among *the radical left* for her strong opinions, and pugilistic manner of expressing them when it comes to the forty-fifth President of the United States. When I type Trump's name into a Facebook search, Facebook auto-fill suggests I may be looking for Cate Gary, The Trumpslayer.

Observing from afar, Donald J. Trump would seem to occupy most of Cate's thoughts over the last year and a half.

"Ha ha. You think I spend an inordinate amount of time thinking about 45?"

I don't. I worry too many of us don't give this disaster of a presidency enough of our time and attention, but the reality of burnout and depression steps in and requires us to take breaks to watch some cute animal videos or maybe indulge in some comics or cartoons that keep the cynicism and nihilism more comfortably vague and abstract. Cate doesn't struggle with this same fatigue.

Even when she does take a break, it's more likely, she explains, that life just got too busy. She assures me she is still thinking of her nemesis. "I just don't have time to get on the phone and compose something that's not just a string of capital letters and obscenities. It takes a little bit of artistry to keep the anti-Trumpism fresh." She remembers that even as an entertainer with a mission, she is still an entertainer.

But what of the ceaseless negativity flowing back toward her? She leaves her posts open to public comment, making herself accessible to Trump trolls around the clock.

"Oh yeah. It's like the walking dead. There's a certain absurdity to them." But the comedian's greatest struggle where the hateful attacks are concerned is just worrying about herself, and whether it's healthy that she finds them so amusing. "We have been taken over by a large group of people who are not intelligent enough to realize how incompetent they are and that they are willingly giving people the tools to their own destruction. I find that hysterical," she says with a laugh. "I'm weird like that. It's a very dark gallows humor to me."

Is there a use to this countertrolling, beyond entertainment? Cate says absolutely, feeling that her egging them on prevents them from maintaining any mask of civility. They show themselves for what they are as they post explosive, hateful screeds at her, full of homophobia, misogyny, and a mind-bogglingly poor grasp of the grammar and spelling rules of the language they want to insist all immigrants speak. Keeping this vitriol on display makes it harder to play down their angry potential.

There are those who take countering the alt-right a step further, like those who, when confronted with a proud and blatant racist like Richard Spencer, respond with a punch to the face. Cate approves. "Heroes! They're the true patriots."

Cate has jokes about the effectiveness and legitimacy (and pleasure) of calling Trump supporters Nazis. So, is it okay to punch anyone in a MAGA hat?

"You know . . . " Cate pauses. "I want to say yes, that's my first impulse [laughing] but I'm thinking, oh, little old lady, so, it's really . . . it depends. Are they also actively endangering people, out there trying to intimidate people? You know, are they like wearing a MAGA hat by a PRIDE parade, and representing that they're going to start some shit?

"Then, yes, punch, punch away. If they're one of the propagandists talking about whatever Richard Spencer calls genocide, you know, like quiet riot or whatever he likes to call it, they're propagating the idea. Punch them, absolutely."

Cate says, with a laugh, she would not go to an Internet Trump supporter's house and punch them in their sleep. "But when they get up, and put their MAGA hat on, and go out and start shit, yeah, then they're punchable."

During the 2016 campaign when Trump referred to Mexican immigrants as being criminals, drug dealers, and rapists, when many immigrants and their allies showed up to throw eggs at Trump supporters and otherwise confront them with what they were supporting and the damage they were attempting to inflict, many of us lost friends if we were unwilling to condemn this.

Cate is unconcerned with the word "Nazi" losing its effectiveness from overuse. "Generations of men have been terrorized into toeing the toxic masculine line for fear of being labeled gay, which means name-calling has a tremendous impact on shaping the culture. So keep calling Nazis Nazis. Let's make the term so widespread that even children in schoolyards start using it against their protofascists."

While I generally stick to discussing the morality of punching Nazis, Cate sees a possible legal justification in the definition of fighting words. She mentions a case where teenager Justin Carter was arrested in Texas for saying on Facebook, sarcastically according to him, that he'd shoot up a kindergarten.

"So, if you piss off white parents, fighting words, the state can bash in your door and take away your freedom. I would apply the same standards to, yeah, you talk shit about Mexican people, he says he's going to rip families apart and deport in record numbers, yeah, fuck yeah, them are fighting words."

It's a great irony that many of the same people who will get upset at you for saying you don't condemn or disagree with these acts of violence will threaten violence in response. Cate has received vague threats, like comments about throwing liberals in ovens, as well as pictures of nooses. "Just pictures of nooses, like I'm gonna fuckin' piss myself. They're very passive-aggressive about it." And she keeps herself ready in case she is doxxed, something she doesn't live in great fear of. "I want to leave this shithole anyways," she says with a laugh. "I'm mentally prepared."

Luckily, and despite the way it sometimes looks, the majority of Trump's online harassment army are not skilled hackers. "I'll be arguing with a Nazi and he'll go to my LinkedIn page and be like, 'Oh, I see you live in San Diego.' And I'm like, 'Yeah, a swing and a miss, fucker.'"

And while she is proud to display her extensive collections of enraged alt-right fanboys, there is a level of anger that can send her reaching for the Block button. "I'm not trying to get murdered."

That she'll meet one of them "in the real world" is of course a real and present danger. As stand-up comedians, our schedules and whereabouts are, by necessity, public. Cate's YouTube videos cheering on "Nazi" as the long-awaited "n-word" you can use to upset white people is seeing a constant inflow of comments, many of them threats. She mostly dismisses the threats as empty, and delivered by cowards acting brave behind keyboards. She describes becoming numb to them after a while. "But I'd be an idiot if I didn't have in the back of my mind that one of them might [make good on their threats]. I'm gonna learn how to fire a gun."

While Cate's partner Robin faces the risk of harassment and violence just for existing openly, her style is considerably less pugnacious. I wonder if she worries about Cate antagonizing such angry and often unhinged people.

"I think she's worried, more worried than she'll let on. But she knows I'm not gonna stop so she tries to be supportive."

It does seem most online threats are idle, as they are hastily made, and if you wait them out, you slowly drop down the troll's enemy list as new names are added hourly. But occasionally things heat up, especially when mobs attack online, egging one another on and rousing one another up, and they doxx, and sometimes, they do in fact kill.

"They're so much fun to rile up, so I'm willing to roll the dice on that," Cate says, dismissing the risks with a shrug and a laugh. And she delights in their angry, over-the-top reactions, collecting screen caps like scalps, each one a notch in her gun. "If they didn't get upset, I'd consider that joke a failure."

Cate understands that not everyone has the same energy and stamina for going one-on-one with the worst people in our society, and she doesn't judge. "Honestly, as long as you're not tap-dancing for Nazis, I try not to judge too harshly. No appeasing, but you don't have to throw a Molotov cocktail into their house, either."

And it's not all hate and veiled threats—Cate is getting her share of fan mail, also. Every day she receives messages from people, many of whom express that they're not in a position to tell their racist brother he's a jackass, or their misogynist boss that he deserves the anger and loneliness that are consuming him, and they're glad that Cate is willing to be their voice.

Does it happen that they occasionally offer a challenging rebuttal, or some satisfying discourse? Not so much. She's getting the same tired and retread arguments. "They'll say 'You use Nazi and it loses its power' or 'You know who the real Nazis are?' and it's Hillary Clinton. I've never been surprised by the freshness of a rebuttal from them, never. I would eat my hat if someone ever said something halfway witty in response."

Comedian Kathy Griffin recently posed a challenge for the Trumpslayer crown when she posted pictures of herself holding Trump's bloody head, causing much uproar, even among liberals. Cate loved it. "Hilarious. I thought when that photo came out that she was doing what I've been hoping someone on the left was gonna do, stepping into the role of Ann Coulter of progressivism. Just straight up, 'I'm going to offend Nazis and with any means possible,' with plausible deniability so you don't get arrested, like finding that line and walking it." Ultimately, though, Griffin stepped away from that line but has not completely disowned it (her current tour utilizes photos in the same outfit holding a globe in place of Trump's head and is titled "The Laughing Your Head Off Tour"). Cate suggests Griffin may have pissed off a Nazi who signs big checks.

Cate does not see Griffin or anyone else who goes after Trump as her competition. In fact, she is glad that harassing Trump and his supporters has become such a popular pastime and welcomes any and all to join the jokers' brigade in resistance to Trump and the alt-right. "Comedy is a wrecking ball. You don't even need to be able to play an instrument, or have any idea about how to pitch your voice. So many people can do it, and we need an army of people doing it."

She is certainly not looking to take Griffin's place. "I don't want to host the New Year's Eve Show. I would rather try to build a following and a career on the path that I'm on now without relying on wealthy Nazis to write my checks."

RADIO RADIO

"Arabs and Muslims are the enemy. They have chosen to be our enemy, and we will not be safe until every Muslim and every Arab and all of their sympathizers in this country are rounded up and put where they can be kept track of. Look, I don't want to see them hurt, I just don't want them to be able to hurt me, or my loved ones, or our American way of life."

I was saying these awful things in a loud and impassioned voice, which was being broadcast throughout the country.

Some months earlier I received a call from a man named Larry. He had been given my number by my friend Brett along with a recommendation that I'd make a good "caller."

Larry hired folks like Brett, a children's entertainer who works under the name Mr. Lizard, to call in to talk radio shows and pretend to be various eccentric characters. Sorry to pull off Santa's beard, but yeah, those outrageous callers they get on your wacky morning show, they're mostly if not totally fake. My guess is the middle man, Larry, is used so they can pretend to believe he is going out and finding actual weirdos, plausible deniability.

I proved I could improvise and do various voices and Larry agreed to put my talents to use. The gig paid fifty dollars a call. The radio show folks would phone me between four and five o'clock in the morning and then put me on hold for an hour or more during which I earned my money, having to listen to their horrible sexist, racist, homophobic ranting until they got to me, the host pretending that I had just dialed in.

In the beginning, Larry wrote the roles for me to play. Not surprisingly, they were crass and infantile. My first time was on *The Mancow Show*. Mancow is a Chicago-based Howard Stern wannabe, twice as creepy and half as clever. I was given the role of "guy who washes his ass with a toothbrush several times a day, and advocates the listening public do the same." I added the detail that I was working on a kid's book. I did research, finding statistics and developing an actual argument. Did you know that over 50 percent of Americans suffer from hemorrhoids? I had no idea.

Mancow didn't need much. After just a few minutes he called me a sick jackass and hung up on me. I barely had a chance to get in, "I'm sick? You sit there with a filthy bum, and you call me sick?"

I played a few more of these horrible characters and then came the abortion call. Larry hired me to play a guy who had spent large amounts of money on fertility treatments trying to have a baby with his new wife only to find out that she had had three abortions prior to their relationship that she had never told him about. This surely meant she was now incapable of getting pregnant.

I made the call. I had a really bad cold that morning, making it easy to sound like I was in tears.

Mancow sympathized completely with me and instructed me to leave that bitch, slut, whore. His callers were less understanding as they slung insults at me in my time of suffering, and more so at my imaginary wife.

I felt like a tool having aided Mancow in this embarrassing misogynistic propaganda. Mancow didn't strike me as pro-life so much as anti–pro-choice, more about hating on his enemy than loving any fetuses. I decided that unless I could ensure better characters, I was done being a caller.

After watching Michael Moore's *Bowling for Columbine*, I had an idea. I called Larry and pitched a new character. He loved it, and I went on Mancow as "Mad Dad," a macho father who was sending his kid to school every day with a gun in his backpack to play hero should any of these "Marilyn Manson freaks" decide to make the school a shooting gallery.

I hoped that by playing the most exaggerated version of the conservative asshole that Mancow represented and appealed to, following his views to their logical extreme, I could push him back the other direction. I said cringeworthy things, like pointing out what lousy shots most of these school shooters were, and how my boy wouldn't get dessert with shooting like that. This strategy worked perfectly, and gun-loving Mancow told gun-loving Mad Dad what a moron he was. This I enjoyed.

The September 11, 2001, attacks happened and I didn't much feel like playing on the radio. But as the backlash against Muslims and Arabs built, I called Larry and pitched an idea for a person who takes this need for security so far, he advocates for all Muslims and Arabs to be placed in internment camps.

Larry went for it, but I wanted to be sure that Mancow would disagree with the caller. I figured he would, but he was extreme enough that I had to be sure.

Larry called the obnoxious talk radio star with me listening on the other line and described the Arab-hating caller.

"God yes. Get him on tomorrow." Mancow was excited.

"So, you disagree with him?" Larry asked.

"What?! Of course I do. He's an asshole!" Mancow answered sharply.

In the wee hours of the morning I had to make as strong of an argument as possible that Arabs should be interned in order to get the response I hoped for.

"Sure, it's easy to say interning the Japanese was wrong, but we won the war, didn't we? We're all better off now, aren't we?"

Mancow went nuts as did his listeners, all of them professing their love for Muslim Americans. I was so delighted at this, it was hard to maintain my angry voice. I was dancing around my living room, bubbling over with excitement.

"Yeah, sure, go ahead and love them from your secured building, Mancow. I don't hear any of them there with you in the studio. Easy for you to love 'em while you stay out of their reach."

"I have a Muslim, Arab woman right here, working the phones!" he snapped back.

"Prove it." Now I really scored. Mancow put a female Arab voice on the radio. She was awesome. She defended her ethnicity and faith and told me off in a language I didn't speak.

Mancow kept me on for over an hour, where I usually got only a couple of minutes. I was still on, yelling terrible racist things as my neighbors began waking and starting their days. I worried that they'd hear me. Brett was on later that day playing another character but was mostly ignored as the Muslim lovefest continued.

I had never felt such pride in my creative endeavors. Larry must have been pleased, as well. He got me on the *Howard Stern Show* next. Unfortunately, I would again be playing a part that

Larry had written for me. Stern interviewed Animal Lover Ben a.k.a. Bestiality Boy, a man trying to create a human dog hybrid by having sex with his neighbor's dogs. Oh well, you win some, you lose some. Stern paid twice what Mancow did and my rent was due.

I would not attempt these kinds of stunts on talk radio today, as, sadly, I'm not at all convinced that modern Trump conservatives would be opposed to the idea of Muslim internment camps or arming schoolchildren.

CIGARS AND CRACKERS

My fourth comedy album came out, and I invited my friend and fellow comic Johnny Taylor Jr. to join me at our neighborhood cigar bar. We planned to smoke our pipes and watch the iTunes charts on our phones, hoping for a good first day response.

We found this particular cigar bar when our friend Michael hosted Joking and Smoking stand-up comedy nights there, and while I knew most of the clientele was more conservative than me, they had a good sense of humor and I always enjoyed performing for them, including the time I'd come by just hoping to have a smoke and watch the show on a rare night off. As I walked in the door, I heard Michael announcing, "Please welcome your next comic, Keith Lowell Jensen." I was confused, but instincts kicked in and I took the stage. As Michael handed me the microphone he whispered, "Twenty minutes," in my ear. I did a twenty-minute set and it went well. It seems one of the comics had been a no-show and Michael was killing time on stage when he saw me come strolling in. It was a room I felt at home in.

Unfortunately, the night of my album release was also the night of the Ferguson riots over the failure of a grand jury to indict police officer Darren Wilson in the shooting death of Michael Brown, an unarmed black man.

Our hearts were heavy from the footage we were seeing from the streets of Ferguson. All the more reason why sitting in a cigar bar and having a mellow night seemed appealing.

Unfortunately, the response to the riots from our fellow smokers was less somber. One man in particular was jovial, and animated, actually walking around the room cracking jokes and explaining how he'd go deal with the "thugs" he believed were "savages" eager for "any excuse to loot and burn down their own communities."

I was honestly trying to hold my tongue. Both Johnny and I had our jaws clenched and I considered politely asking if we could change the subject, but when I heard the big jolly cigar-chomping man say, "They need to send in the Reserves and just arrest everyone on the streets, let them know this shit don't stand," I finally snapped.

"Maybe a more practical idea is for cops to stop killing black people."

The whole room got quiet. Johnny tightened his hands into fists.

"What did you say?"

We yelled back and forth at each other, and it was clear that Johnny was the one and only person there who didn't think I was completely out of line. One of the older cigar-chompers told me he had black grandchildren. I somehow managed not to reply, "Yeah? Well so did Thomas Jefferson and Strom Thurmond."

Michael, my dear friend who'd introduced me to this smoke shop, would later write me to say, "I worried this might happen when I saw your Facebook post that you were going to a cigar bar where most of the customers are cops." I had no idea this was a cop hangout. This was information Michael could have shared with me sooner.

Continuing to argue with my fellow smokers, things got more heated, and finally I told the big cracker piece of shit that he was a big cracker piece of shit and did my best to break down empirically what it was that made him a big cracker piece of shit.

He said, "Boy, you're about to get your ass kicked!"

I saw Johnny getting ready to fight. I rose to my feet and yelled back, "REALLY?! REALLY?! That's all it takes to get you to resort to violence? Some smart-ass talking shit in a cigar bar and you're ready to get violent, and you've got the fucking nerve to condemn their being violent when they're getting shot in the street!" I waited, still pretty sure that I was about to get my ass kicked.

To my absolute amazement, big cracker says, "That's a good point . . . you just saved yourself from an ass whooping."

I quit smoking tobacco a short time later.

Police continue to kill black people.

"Nazi Punks! Nazi Punks! Nazi Punks . . . Oh, you have a permit. I see. Well, okay, sorry. Carry on then."

—Not the Dead Kennedys

A CHAPTER FOR WHITE PEOPLE

alling a quick white people meeting here. I know those are
usually bad, but trust me, no white hoods or anything, just
gotta chat with my fellow whities for a minute.

We would-be good guys are spending way too much time and
energy in-fighting, and there are a few key things I see us go at
one another on again and again. The good news is, on each of
these issues I'm right, and you're wrong, and we just need to get
that clear and we'll be able to move on to fighting the good fight.
Easy enough, yeah?

Once you're also right, you need to help spread the truth even
to your asshole friends, especially to your asshole friends, now
that you're no longer an asshole. You're welcome for that, by the
way. Well worth the price of this book, I'd say (that and the story
about my friend Ben's parents doing anal on camera).

Look, I know it feels good to tell someone to fuck off for saying
racist shit. It can make you feel like one of the good ones, an ally.
Unfortunately, it's often the opposite of what we white people

ought to be doing. "Wha?! How could this be? Mr. Punch-a-Nazi would deprive me of the joy of unfriending, blocking, banning, and openly mocking a racist?"

Yeah. Sorry.

What's a racist? I mean, we're all racist, which is to say it's something we should all struggle with and work against, but "a racist"? We tend to reserve this word for the blatant racist, the dedicated, actively racist person who will proudly talk about serving and preserving their race, which they simultaneously think is both superior and on the verge of being done in by natural selection. I personally don't find trying to convert these dudes a judicious use of time or resources, as there is way too little pay off.

The "racists" we deal with more often in our own social circles are would-be allies, well-intentioned souls, who are asking honest questions and just don't know what the fuck they're talking about. Don't get me wrong, I don't expect any black person to be patient with their "I'm just asking questions" nonsense, but I do expect this patience of myself. Admittedly, I am terrible at it.

A refrain I've been hearing of late is "Hey, white people, come get your boy," which I take to mean, "I already answered your asinine questions that time you drank too much and wanted to have a heart-to-heart when I was just trying to relax, now you talk to this dude. Pay that knowledge forward." Though sometimes it means "Your uncle is a drunk racist asshole. Deal with him. I'm trying to have a good time at this party."

We should at least try to answer the questions that they're just asking, if they seem to be asking them sincerely, and not using the Socratic method to try to drive their point home because they have so much to teach the world about "the real racism." If their intentions really are pure, and they're at all willing to listen, we should talk to 'em.

And of course sometimes you get to be the clueless white ally. Lord knows I have been. Thanks to my black friends who've been patient with me, and thanks to white friends who have taken a deep breath and helped me when I'd pushed the patience of said black friends too far and they had to call someone to come get their boy. The last time I just-asking-questions-ed a friendship to death, it was with a comedian who I respect tremendously and the story ended up in his act. I'm wondering if I can use it on my résumé as a TV credit. (We've since had a cup of coffee and a hug, but the friendship isn't what it was.)

I've included this chapter to address a few stumbling blocks I've seen would-be allies get hung up on. Of course this is a white dude's perspective on these issues hoping to help you catch up a bit. I'm like the piano teacher who is trying to stay one lesson ahead of her student.

Ultimately of course, if you want to hear about black people stuff, you should read some black authors, you wanna hear about women stuff, you need to read some women, if you want to hear about gay people stuff, I think you get the point, they all write books too, and think pieces, and articles for *Huff Po*, *Teen Vogue*, or *Ebony*, and funny memes, and poems, and songs, and movies, and damn, now I'm getting excited. I won't fault you if you just skip this chapter and go straight to the source or *The Source*, a fine publication.

PRIVILEGE

Privilege can be a real difficult thing for some people to grasp, particularly whites who grew up poor, or in other harsh circumstances.

People struggle with the concept that you can have racial privilege and not have economic/class privilege. You can be the son of addicts living in poverty, and you're still the white, male son of addicts living in poverty, which doesn't mean you don't have a hell of a hard lot in life, if anything it's all the more reason you should have some compassion for people that don't have that gender or racial privilege.

I came across a Dust Bowl–era photo of two white children of coal miners, with big eyes and dirty clothes and faces, and someone had captioned it "Go ahead, tell them they're privileged." I guess the author of the meme (memer? Sir Memes-a-Lot?) didn't stop to think, if these white kids have it this bad, what are the odds that their black neighbors have it better? Or even as good? Are they imagining a black man owns the mine?

From my white friends who didn't grow up poor I hear, "Oh, so I should feel guilty because I have a decent job, and place to live? I worked hard for this."

Of course you shouldn't feel bad for what you have. The good things you have because of your privilege are mostly okay. It's not bad that you have them, it's bad that having them is a privilege, and that that privilege might in any way be afforded to you because of your skin color, gender, religion, sexuality, etc. You should only feel bad if you're somehow managing to not notice or care that other people working just as hard aren't doing quite as well. It's probably not your fault it's happening, but who else is to blame for you not giving a shit about it? And that is what privilege means, by the way: even outside of discussions of race, privilege doesn't mean a good thing, it means a good thing awarded to a specific person or group of people.

I didn't hear white privilege talked about much when I was younger. I'll admit, I had a hard time with it at first, too. But I've come to realize, talking about privilege is actually very generous. It's not just labeling a person who has said or done something

216

racist a racist, but rather looking at where their views and misunderstandings may be coming from. It's saying, "Look, you're not *necessarily* a fool, you just lack a certain perspective." Check your privilege is a pretty friendly way to say, "Sssssshhhhh. This might be one of those times to listen to people who actually experience the shit we're discussing."

I had a heated argument one night about privilege, and a friend kept pointing out that it was I who was privileged. He pointed out my newish sneakers, my "hipster pants" (maybe the only time my thirty-three dollar Wrangler Wranchers have ever gotten the respect they deserve). I kept agreeing with him. I couldn't seem to make him understand that I wasn't saying otherwise. I was imploring us all to recognize our privilege, myself included, and to believe people of color when they tell us what it's actually like for them in this culture. They've been writing about it in novels, poems, and stand-up comedy sets, singing about it, rapping about it, for ages, and it wasn't until they were able to start filming it that we actually started to believe them, and some of us are still holding out.

I've heard the argument that black people and white people are equally racist. So much to unpack there, but even if this were true, and that simple, and black people and white people were equally racist, there are way more of us. That would still put us at a HUGE advantage in dealing with racism in this society.

Black people can't be racist.
This one has broken up some friendships for sure. Here's how I take it when I hear that only white people can be racist. When we talk about racism, when we're discussing racism as a problem, it's shorthand for systemic racism. Systemic racism is the problem, after all. I mean, some people not liking other people

217

based on their skin color sucks for sure, but it's a bigger problem when it's systemic, widespread enough to thwart the groups in the minority, and advantage those in the majority. That's the racism we're confronting, which is oppressing and keeping people down. If you're white, you may feel bigotry (and I sincerely hope you get to experience being in the minority sometime even for a day; it's a microcosm but still a real eye-opener), but you are securely in the majority in the United States. Yes, you are. No, you are. No, you won't be a minority in a few years. That's only if you count every minority group together, as one group. All of them combined may soon outnumber Caucasians, but we will remain the largest ethnic group for quite some time. Shut up with that bullshit. Goddammit, I'm sorry. Look, I warned you I was bad at this.

Look, I've had bigoted speech aimed at me based on the color of my skin.

I was standing in line at an amusement park, Disneyland or Knott's Berry Farm, I don't remember which. I was very young, maybe single digits. A group of black girls were cutting in line, and as they pushed past me racing toward the front, I protested, "Hey!"

One of the girls yelled back at me, "Fuck you, white shit," and they continued on their way to the front of the line.

It hurt. It stung, badly enough that almost four decades later a full-grown man still remembers it. I was taught by my parents and teachers that racism was the worst thing, and an accidental part of that lesson was that black people were inherently champions of racial harmony. It was wrong that that girl said that to me. My feelings of hurt were valid.

But, when she said these hurtful words to me, it was shocking. To be shocked was itself a privilege. There was not a lifelong history of me questioning my worth because I was white and had words like this aimed at me every day. This wasn't one in a long series of incidents of me being put down for the color of my skin. My ethnic history was presented to me as Vikings on one side, kilts and bagpipes on the other, coming to America, not one of my people being dragged here in bondage. And I was surrounded by other white people as I felt this hurt. I wasn't a lone white face in a sea of darker faces feeling alone in my anger and betrayal. I didn't watch movies and cartoons every day full of faces that didn't resemble my own. There was little to no chance that an authority figure at the park was going to take her side based on her being black and me being white.

So yeah, it was wrong and it fits a definition of racism, but it isn't what we talk about when we discuss the racism that people of color deal with, the racism that we struggle with as a culture. It doesn't help that cause, it certainly hurts it, and it sucks but it's not the same struggle, not even close.

That little girl was being an asshole. I wish I could thank her for giving me a tiny, little glimpse at what it feels like to be made to feel bad about the color of your skin, and years later helping me understand just how tiny that glimpse was.

I don't see color; race doesn't exist; you're the racist for being aware of race at all.

I've seen quite a few takes on this. In the atheist circles I often run in, I get this "rational" approach, "Race is a human construct. It doesn't matter. It doesn't exist." This is actually valuable if you're talking to a hardcore blatant racist who wants to argue that one race is genetically superior to another. But I don't waste a lot of time on those assholes. Unfortunately, I see this logic being erroneously applied to argue against people fighting for empowerment, or against things like appropriation, and white-washing. It's often accompanied by "Sorry, I just judge individuals as individuals, and not by the color of their skin. Who's the real racist here?"

It's them of course. Judging people as individuals is great, but we should also be aware that until all of society does that, which we're a long way from, people of different skin colors will have different experiences, struggles, and ethnic identities based on how said society treats them.

As far as the science goes, race being a poor way to organize us genetically doesn't mean it doesn't exist. Race being a human construct doesn't mean it doesn't exist. Don't pull over for the police when they turn their lights and sirens on behind you. After all, "police" is a human construct. Genetically speaking, a police officer is just another human. And don't worry about his gun, it's a human construct, too. Why make sure your doctor has a medical degree? Talk about a human construct. It's not like that degree means she has a specific set of experiences that might see her more qualified to speak on certain topics, like your health for instance.

Being color-blind may seem like a good goal, but it often means that instead of not seeing race, you're not seeing racism. And when a person of color is talking to you about race, you should see color, and you should listen to them.

Yeah, well, you're a harsher judge of straight, white males than you are of anyone else.
Yep.

Are you saying I am looking at the group I'm a member of with a more critical eye? And you're not praising me for this? Weird, since I hear black people being told all the time that this is what they should be doing.

You're just trying to be politically correct.

Yep, again.

As a comedian I get this one a lot. Correct is a nice word, right? Which part of the phrase politically correct sounds like a bad thing to you?

Political correctness and comedy became a talking point again when Jerry Seinfeld announced he no longer felt he could play colleges, as if his observations about socks in washer machines were going to enrage the kids.

I don't give a fuck that Jerry Seinfeld (who I admire greatly, for the record) can't play colleges anymore. I don't weep for him any more than I would for Frank Sinatra when Elvis took over, or Elvis when the Beatles came along. Oh no, the kids have changing taste and values and have new favorites, the world is ending!

Let me tell you a sad story. There was once a comedian who had to give up his act because of the damn PC police. Yeah! He was the last of his kind, and it broke his heart to have to stop making people laugh because the politically correct liberals had no damn sense of humor. Aren't you feeling terrible for him? His heart was heavy, and tears mixed with his "blackface" makeup as he prepared to remove it after his last show. Poor guy. Oh well, at least he could still tell gay jokes.

Ironically, politically correct is yet another phrase co-opted by the right in their Orwellian way. Originally the complaint was about terms like friendly fire, and conflict, in place of involuntary manslaughter, and war. Now it's about white dudes getting grief for saying the n-word.

People of color, listen to me, I'm a white guy who knows how to end racism!

So many armchair quarterbacks in the ending racism game. They usually have advice after something terrible happens and there is a violent response: "Violence isn't the way to solve this." And that's a reasonable point of view. I certainly know black people who feel this way. But you know what, until you're on the front line of fighting racism yourself, maybe don't be trying to call the shots. Maybe focus more on the racism, not the victims of racism's response to it.

"If you want to end racism just stop focusing so much on race. You're only adding to the problem." I am amazed that this one is still out there, but it is, and I still hear it on a regular basis. What problem goes away if you don't pay attention to it? Oh yeah, any problem that isn't affecting you personally. Oddly enough, when people of color ignore race, they're still discriminated against by banks, law enforcement, the justice system, and employers.

I don't want to get caught up in judging the quality of the advice, because the point is, it's not our place as white people to be giving advice to black people on how to deal with white racism. You want to help, ask how you can help. Shy? There are books, podcasts, blogs, documentaries by people of color about the struggle for equality, its history, philosophy, and even specifically the role of white people in the movement, which from what I see is mostly in a support role, and in taking some responsibility to talk to our white neighbors, friends, and family.

And now for a weird analogy: You notice black hip-hop artists mostly give respect to Eminem? Yeah, that's because he is in that game full-time, and he worked his way up. He paid dues, and he paid respect, and now, it seems, he can talk about rap with some authority. When you're barely, or not at all, involved in the struggle for civil rights, you sound like Vanilla Ice telling black people, women, gay people, or anyone else who deals with this shit everyday how they should be doing it. Those nonviolent actions you think they should be doing, shut up and go do them!

APPROPRIATION

Musical pioneer Thelonious Monk said the following about the creation of be-bop during a time when white band leaders had come to dominate jazz: "We wanted a music that they couldn't play."

Don't confuse appropriation with collaboration amongst equals. They're not the same thing.

Everyday Sunshine is a great documentary on one of my favorite bands, Fishbone, true innovators and a huge influence on bands like No Doubt, Sublime, Red Hot Chili Peppers, and the whole nineties third-wave ska scene (but don't hold that against them). Throughout the film, millionaire white artist after millionaire white artist enthusiastically tell the cameras that they owe so much to Fishbone. Then, the cameras cut to members of Fishbone, struggling to get by, frontman Angelo moving back in with his mom. I couldn't help but think, *If you owe them so much, could you maybe write a check?*

Yes, as artists we are gonna influence one another, but there is a long history of black innovators getting less credit (and less money) than white imitators. There is a right and a wrong way to collaborate, and staying aware of this history, realizing the system is rigged, and trying not to perpetuate that is the responsibility of any artist who respects the artistic community, and his fellow humans.

And then there are the things that just aren't up for grabs. For example, Native American headdresses mean something to Native

Americans. I'm not gonna speak for them. Perhaps they had a big ceremony granting you their blessing to wear a headdress. Unless you're sure they're cool with it, though, maybe don't.

I'm not saying you don't have a legal right to wear 'em. I'm saying, know that it may be disrespectful and hurtful, and the oft-stated goal of honoring or paying tribute doesn't hold water if the people you're honoring specifically don't want you doing the thing you're doing.

Also, we're all so tired of hearing about your legal rights. If "Well, it isn't illegal" is the best defense you have, you're coming from a pretty weak moral position.

I chose the headdress as one example trusting you could extrapolate from there. (Fuck your blonde dreadlocks [full disclosure; I once had blonde dreadlocks].)

I'M NOT A RACIST!

I am a racist, but I'm trying hard every day not to be.

Goddamn, we white people hate being called a racist, or even feeling like we're being called a racist. I have seen white people get so mad at being accused of being racist they start saying racist shit. If you ever feel like saying, "I'm not a racist," do yourself a favor, stop and look at the racism you're being accused of instead. Actually address the action or speech being criticized, maybe not even with the person pointing it out to you, maybe with someone you trust who knows where your heart is at. It'd be real nice to hear more of us saying, "Oh! Sorry. Didn't mean to be racist," which will go way further toward proving you're not a racist than saying, I'm Not a Racist. In fact, sometimes I think "I'm not a racist" is the mating call of the North American Racist. "I'm not a racist" has oddly become a kind of racist dog whistle.

And besides, who wants to settle for not being a blatant racist? In this day and age we should be striving to be antiracists.

You don't have to agree with anything in this chapter, but if you want a less racist planet, you can't let any of these sticking points stop you from chasing the goal daily in your speech and actions. We're all counting on you.

A HELPFUL GLOSSARY OF MODERN TERMS FROM THE RIGHT

Alt-right: Conservatives who don't bother even trying to hide their racism.

Cosmopolitan: Jewish.

Cuck: Just a new way to say henpecked/pussy-whipped. What you call dudes who give a fuck about the well-being of women.

I just tell it like it is: The concept of tact evades me.

Libtard: Liberal, but you know, with 'tard added, because so clever.

Modern presidential: Completely unpresidential.

Not a racist but . . .: A racist.

NuMale: With every minute that passes since the last time you smashed a beer can on your forehead, you can with increasing accuracy be described as a NuMale. See also: Cuck.

Politically correct: What you call one who is any distance, great or small, ahead of you in terms of respecting others. Going further than just not calling people the n-word, or, for some, going so far as not calling people the n-word.

Racial realist: Racist who likes *Star Trek*.

Snowflake: Sensitive, but lacking compassion for the average alt-right troll's sensitivity, including their sensitivity to sensitivity.

Social justice warrior: Passionately compassionate toward other people.

Socially liberal, fiscally conservative: I like justice and equality, sure, I just like money more.

Thug: TV-friendly n-word.

Urban: Black.

White guilt: Derogatory for white responsibility or even white awareness.

SHERIE, ROCK AND ROLL, AND MEYER LANSKY CRACKING NAZI SKULLS

Getting kicked out of my high school and having to go to Success Continuation High School is one of the best things that ever happened to me. That is where I met a teacher who would teach me so much more than the curriculum she'd been assigned by the state.

Sherie (we called our teachers by their first names) taught English, and a class of her own design called "Self-Esteem." She introduced us kids to the idea that liking yourself was not only a worthwhile goal, but something you could actually do something about. Her classes were way off the beaten track, with guided visualization, students subjecting one another to their favorite music and discussing why they hated one another's favorite music—I seem to remember some sage being burnt from time to time.

Whatever subject Sherie taught she managed to work in some real talk on civil rights. As a young woman in the sixties, Sherie answered the call of Martin Luther King Jr., leaving her parents' comfortable house in the white suburbs to go to the Deep South and help register black people to vote. She put her life on the line, dealing with violence and death threats. I make it a point to thank her for her service every Veterans Day. Eventually she came back to California and continued to do good work, trying to teach us mostly white kids how to not be shitty people.

We watched several music documentaries in Sherie's class. A good doc on American music IS a civil rights documentary. Jazz, rock and roll, doo wop, soul, funk, hip-hop—the African American Civil Rights Movement has the best soundtrack.

I'd watch these documentaries with great enthusiasm. They would always include an interview with some old racist gas station owner who didn't want to hear that "black music." White kids listening to black music was a slippery slope, he'd warn. It would lead to white kids dancing to black music! And this would lead to interracial dancing, which would lead to interracial dating, which would lead to interracial mating, which would lead to fire and brimstone and Satan and polyester blends and the end of civilization as we know it! My wish whenever I see one of these old racists talking about the slippery slope is that they were blessed with good health and led a good long life. I hope with all my might that they lived long enough to see that they were right. I love the idea of them on their deathbed being comforted by their lovely, blonde-haired, blue-eyed granddaughter, and her lovely, black, transgender wife.

But I'd also settle for, they died miserable and alone.

I think of these documentaries often, and I ask myself who I want to be in the documentaries of my time. I don't want to be the scared old gas station owner trying to stop the world from spinning. But I don't want to be the person who isn't worth including in the documentary, either. I want to be one of those who stood up for the right thing at the right time.

And when it comes to violence, history shines brightly on those who stood up to tyranny and bigotry. Even abolitionist John Brown is a controversial figure at worst, but increasingly he is looked at as a hero, and certainly held in higher regard than the vile slave masters he targeted. Of course those who fought and won the Civil War are held in high regard. Violence is unquestionably acceptable when you have a uniform, and you win.

Meyer Lansky was a notorious Jewish gangster. He was a criminal, but even this criminal's story has a bright spot, thanks to a bit of righteous violence. As Hitler and his Nazis rose in power in Germany, they had support in the United States from a group that called themselves The German American Bund.

In an article attributed to Sadie The Goat on AnarchoGeekReview.com, I found the delightful story of Lansky being asked, by judge, politician, and fellow Jew, Nathan D. Perlman, to go and beat some Nazi ass, for a reasonable fee of course. Lansky agreed to deliver the beatings but refused Perlman's money. His Nazi punching would be done pro bono. Captain America is cool, and I love the Nazi punching prowess shown by Indiana Jones, but no fictional superhero Nazi puncher can come close to topping the coolness of a real-life Jewish wise guy roughing up American Nazis. Lansky not only punched Nazis, he trained other Nazi punchers. I love the idea of a Nazi punching workshop. "When you see a Nazi, will you be ready to punch them? Come get some solid Nazi punching techniques from experts in the field."

Even my most ardently anti-Nazi punching friends can't help but admire the story of yesterday's Nazis taking a thrashing from a bunch of Jewish gangsters.

Did the media at the time wonder about these Nazis' freedom of speech? Did they wring their hands worrying about civil discourse with Nazis? Did they think it was an overreaction to something that didn't present a real threat? Journalist Walter Winchell did not: he cheered Lansky on as he spread the news of the Bund's meetings being interrupted.

When they look back at our current period of white nationalism again rearing its ugly head and gaining ground, I hope it will be to report on a failed attempt foiled by people taking it seriously, not waiting for the police or the courts, but just standing up for their neighbors and themselves and saying, "No! Not on my street. Not on my campus. Not in my government. Never again!"

I don't think I'm in any position to be a Meyer Lansky in this story, but I can at least be Walter Winchell. Who do you want to be?

IN CONCLUSION

Punch Nazis.

ACKNOWLEDGMENTS

Thanks to: Chris Cubas, Ngaio Bealum, Cate Gary, and Dan Arel, for loaning me their great words on the merits of punching Nazis.

Monty Neysmith, Dennis Yudt, Cate Gary, and Farty McFuckbutt for sitting for intereviews.

Sherie Labedis, you put your own life in harm's way to fight white supremacy, and you taught your teenage students year after year that justice was a thing to fight for.

Shon Meckfessel for loaning me your ears and brains and talking me through some of this.

W. Kamau Bell for teaching me lessons you'd assumed I'd already learned.

The Coup, for keeping the revolution funky.

Sadie the Goat on AnarchoGeekReview.com, thanks for hipping me to Meyer Lansky's Nazi beating side.

Alex Hess for editing the fuck out of this mess.

Carrie Poppy for having the ridiculous idea that I could write a book in the first place.

Don Letts and the BBC4 documentary *The Story of Skinhead*.

I worked out parts of this manuscripts at Cobbs and The Punch Line in San Francisco, Luna's, The Comedy Spot, and The Punch Line in Sacramento, and at many other bars, clubs, cafes, and galleries around the US. Thanks for letting me ramble on about Nazi punching on your stages.

My wife and my kid gave me many hours of almost-quiet time to work on this.

Thanks Uncle Harold for being willing to tell me, and anyone else, when they appear to be full of shit.

Cate Gary, Robin Tran, Johnny Taylor, Becky Lynn, Aaron Carnes, Julie Lynn, Arielle Robbins, and anyone else who looked at this and talked to me about it, thank you.

Typed on Jim Fourniadis laptop. Thanks, Jim.